THE
SELF - SUPPORTING
CITY

by

GILBERT M. TUCKER

A completely rewritten and revised edition
published in response to continuing demand.

1958
Robert Schalkenbach Foundation
New York

ACKNOWLEDGMENT

The following conversation between William H. Seward, Secretary of State under Lincoln, and Andrew H. Green, a distinguished citizen of New York, is recorded in the book, *A War-Time Statesman*, by Mr. Seward's son.

Taking up a corporation report, Mr. Seward said:

"Mr. Green, here is something which you can comprehend but I confess I cannot. Here is a great corporation which, by its report, shows it is well managed and profitable and pays all its expenses.

"Now, the city of New York is a corporation which has vastly more property and resources in the way of real estate, streets, franchises, docks and wharves, buildings, rents, licenses, powers and privileges, than any other corporation possibly can have. And yet it cannot pay its own expenses! It has to ask the individual taxpayer to go down into his pockets and take out of his personal earnings a yearly contribution, in order to keep this gigantic corporation on its feet. Why should not the city of New York pay its own expenses? Why should the individual taxpayer be called upon at all?"

To this Mr. Green replied:

"Mr. Seward, you are right. The problem is one that I have worked on over many years. The city of New York has given away more than enough to pay its expenses many times over. But the citizens of New York don't see it, either because they are too careless, or too ignorant, or too unpatriotic, or don't care. Whichever it is, the fact remains that they don't correct it, or don't want to."

To Lady Gosford, who called attention to this conversation, and to the *Herald Tribune*, which published her letter under the heading, "A Self Supporting City," thereby suggesting a title, acknowledgment is due.

PREFACE

The author's aim is to discuss broad and general principles, attempting to show the wisdom of the policy and the plan which he advocates but not to formulate a program of legislation. One reader of the manuscript raises objection to our proposals saying that they would be illegal. Of course they would be, and the problem is to make them legal by the necessary legislation, but just what legislation is called for, and how it should be drawn, is aside from our purpose and depends upon state and city laws already on the books.

Conditions are very different in different states, and even in different cities, and it would be futile to enter into any detailed discussion. Even when specific cities are cited we make no attempt to formulate laws but suggest only a general plan of action, without even studying existing statutes.

If some readers feel that this betokens impracticability we can only say that we refuse to accept such a defeatist position. What we advocate is already partially achieved and is being increasingly recognized. Denmark, Australia and many small countries have accepted much of what we advocate. In more than half of our states a program of tax exemption for new industries has long been in effect with good results. Sometimes this is legally established and sometimes it is extra-legal but, however that may be, it has proved so beneficial and successful there is little inclination to abandon it where it has been tried.

By a program of tax exemption Puerto Rico has completely changed the life of the little island. From a backward agricultural economy, cursed with dire poverty, they have developed a modern, progressive industrial life and have recently celebrated the establishment of their four-hundredth industrial plant. This change in the way of life has raised the average annual family income from $660 to $2360, and this has been accomplished very largely through tax reform. We note in a current magazine a two-page spread advertisement headed "Why 402 U. S. Manufacturers Enjoy 100% Tax Freedom in Puerto Rico." We are told that recently this program shows signs of failing, for tax exemption granted only temporarily as bait, is now running out in many cases and industry is closing up or moving away. This only strengthens our case: when there was full exemption, there was prosperity but as industry is taxed, it dies or moves away.

If objection is raised to the changes suggested in assessment methods, remember that today recognized assessment practices are often in violation of law. Frequently, by legal authority or by common consent, land value is assessed at only a small percentage of what the

law demands and frequently land values are assessed at one percentage of the true figure, improvement values at another percentage, and nothing at the value which the law demands. The assessor's oath to assess property at full value is usually an absolute travesty.

That it is not too difficult to secure legislative action is shown by experience. In Pennsylvania Pittsburgh and Scranton long ago took a big step toward our objective with benefit so generally recognized that it opened the door to legislation permitting similar change in the other cities of the State. The legislation was carried unanimously in the Senate, with only an occasional dissenting voice in the Lower House.

There is a general impression that real estate interests and land speculators would oppose the plan but experience in Pennsylvania shows that this opposition is greatly exaggerated. There are always a few dyed-in-the-wool land gamblers who oppose any change but it is not difficult to make most real-estate operators see the wisdom of the plan. Practically always, when city realty changes hands, the transaction is prompted by desire to improve the property, to build, to re-build, or to modernize, and all such operations are made far easier and far more profitable under our plan than today. If we are ever to have a rational plan of city taxation and we are to do away with slums, fire hazards, housing problems and vicious living conditions, acceptance of this plan is imperative.

A survey, proposed and sponsored by the Economic Education League, has recently been completed by the Institute of Research of Lehigh University, covering the city of Bethlehem, Pa. This study was excellently planned and conducted by the University experts, with no interference from any outside source. It is nonpolitical and without bias or prejudice and is purely factual. This survey is the first of its kind made by competent trained research analysts, to the best of our knowledge and belief, and it will undoubtedly blaze the way for similar studies, three of which are already in the planning stage.

We believe that conditions are acute and that the American public are generally aware of the needs of stabilizing public finances, reducing tax burdens at the same time, and making our cities better and healthier and housing our people more comfortably. These housing needs should be met in a way which relieves and does not impose burdens on the taxpayers. An object of this little book is to make it clear how this may be accomplished and how much can be achieved without resorting to socialistic or communistic housing, paid for by some to supply homes to others. We believe that it is easily possible to make our cities self-supporting units, meeting their expenses by the earnings of the city.

CONTENTS

THE SELF-SUPPORTING CITY

The City Throws Away Its Investments, Resorts to Taxation, and Goes on the Rocks

Municipal taxation as now levied can and should be a thing of the past: the American city can be a self-supporting corporation, meeting its expenses from its rightful income. Taxation is unnecessary, because the city has, in its physical properties, acquired through the years, by the expenditure of its people's moneys, a huge capital investment from which it collects only a very small part of the return earned. In streets, pavements, water supply, sewers, transit facilities, parks, playgrounds, schools and libraries; in equipment of the protective services of police, fire and sanitation, and in a hundred things, it has invested much. Little of the interest which this investment might earn finds its way back into the municipal treasury, and a large part of the value is destroyed by a system which prevents utilization of the benefits. Where would a business stand were its capital investment to earn nothing, leaving it dependent upon assessments against the owners? Of course city finances are headed for the rocks.

At one time a billion dollars of municipal bonds were in default, and some placed the figure three times as high. Municipalities in trouble numbered 851, counties and school districts about 1,000, and miscellaneous districts about 400. Actually the situation was worse than defaulted indebtedness shows, for, even when some obligations continue to be met, repudiation or delay in facing any obligation indicates that the debtor is in trouble and jeopardizes his credit. A man may have a few trivial judgments against him, but even these often forebode a grievous crash. The debts of cities of over five thousand population, aggregating almost two and a quarter billion dollars, were at least partially in default and, of the larger cities, 269 in ten states had failed to meet their obligations.

Much of this insolvency is caused by reckless spending for unsound projects engineered by speculator-promoters. There have been difficulties in such cities as New York, Chicago, and Detroit, usually after sprees of extravagance. Detroit probably held the record, finding it necessary to effect compromise adjustments on indebtedness of some $400,000,000. Today New York City is in a precarious position with little relief in sight. No wonder municipal financing is a headache, with many a city on the edge of insolvency, and there is every reason to see added difficulties with conditions which coming years will bring.

Were the city to collect a just return on its assets it would be on the way to stability, security, and corporate prosperity. Judging future capital expenditures by probability of earnings, as we do in business, the city would forge rapidly ahead and could do much which would be wise and beneficial, instead of being sometimes held back by pressure of political expediency. No longer would we be saddled with bond issues to "pay for dead horses"; borrowings for sound projects would be self-liquidating and a crushing load would be lifted from the shoulders of the inhabitants. It is necessary only to recapture the city's rightful income, and how this may be done equitably we shall show.

Financial benefit from improvements made by the city accrues almost wholly to the advantage of landowners; but, while this is incontrovertible, the fact remains that landowners seldom prosper and are often in dire straits. They send up a constant and justifiable wail of lamentation and, in thousands of cases, the value of their holdings completely disappears and properties are lost by forfeiture. We give landowners much, but they are ruined; we lavish benefits upon them, but they do not prosper. How can this paradox be explained?

The answer is simple: we must make it possible to put land to profitable use. Urban land seldom brings in much but tax bills, unless built upon; and, if building is profitless, the site itself loses value, as evidenced by forfeiture of many holdings unable to meet tax costs. It is a vicious chain. First we create value in land; then, by taxing it inadequately, we give much of this value away. Finally, by oppressive taxation of buildings, we prevent the profitable utilization of what the city provides, destroying potential value created.

The predicament of the city is entangled with the troubles of landowners; and, since cities depend on real estate taxation for most of their income, landowners and city suffer together. The two interests cannot be separated. We must restore lost values to realty, we must recapture the income which belongs to the city, and we must untax the buildings which are justly private property, thus making it profitable to put landholdings to productive use, no longer letting each rob the other. For this double robbery there is a simple remedy, but first let us see how values created and paid for by all are given away and ultimately wiped out, leaving the pockets of landowners empty and the city confronted with a steadily shrinking tax base.

How the Public Improvements Benefit Landowners Who Nevertheless Do Not Prosper

It is common knowledge that wise public improvements and the extension of the services of government add substantially to the value of the land. New streets, pavements, boulevards, parks, schools and better protection at the hands of fire, police and health departments all increase land values in favored sections. Even before such improvements are made — often when only tentatively proposed — there is an upsurge in the prices at which land is held, and great and far-reaching developments bring sensational advances.

The effect of the West Side I.R.T. subway in New York is shown in a most painstaking study made by a committee of the City Club, under the leadership of Colonel Homer Folks. Since the effect was relatively slight downtown where transportation needs were already met, we confine a summary of the findings to uptown and semi-surburban areas which reaped the greater benefit. The report makes allowances for increment in land values resulting from normal growth of the city, so by subtracting the increase in the previous seven years from the increase in the seven years which marked the opening of the subway, we have the enhancement brought about by that alone.

From 135th Street to Spuyten Duyvil the rise in land values in these seven years was $69,300,000. Subtracting the normal increase during the previous seven years — $20,100,000 — leaves an increase of $49,200,000 directly attributable to the opening of the line. Had the landowners in this area paid the entire cost of that section of the subway — $7,375,000 — they would still have had a net profit in the increased value of their holdings, resulting solely from its construction, of $41,825,000, or 89 per cent.

In the Bronx the increase was $44,800,000. Again subtracting the normal enhancement of values of $13,500,000, we have a net profit of $31,300,000, brought about by the subway. The cost of this section was $5,700,000, and had those who directly benefited paid the bill, there would have remained a net profit of $25,600,000, or almost double the normal rise. The cost of the entire subway, from its start at the Battery to its upper reaches in the Bronx, was about $43,000,000. Had this been borne by the landowners in favored areas who reaped the benefit, they would still have had a net profit of $37,500,000.

A similar instance is offered by the George Washington Bridge across the Hudson, which an official declared increased New Jersey land values by some $300,000,000, or more than six times its cost. As this book is in process of revision, the daily press reports enormous increases in the value of lands peculiarly benefited by the opening of the New York State Thruway, particularly in outlying sections of certain cities. The value of some holdings, which profit greatly by improved transportation facilities, is multiplied many times. These illustrations show how such undertakings bring enormous profit to landowners. Is there any valid reason why such improvements should not be assessed against properties benefited? They more than pay for themselves and could be made self-supporting, self-liquidating and often very profitable.

Winston Churchill Cites Examples

In contrast to these great enterprises take a trivial but comparable example cited by Winston Churchill in a speech delivered at King's Theatre, Edinburgh, on July 17, 1909:

"Some years ago there was a toll-bar on a bridge across the Thames, and all the working people who lived on the south side of the river had to pay a daily toll of one penny for going and returning from their work. The spectacle of these poor people thus mulcted of so large a proportion of their earnings appealed to the public conscience, an agitation was set on foot, municipal authorities were roused, and at the cost of the ratepayers the bridge was freed and the toll removed. All those people who used the bridge were saved sixpence a week. Within a very short period from that time the rents on the south side of the river were found to have advanced by about sixpence a week, or the amount of the toll which was remitted."

But it is not only from officially financed operations that such results ensue. Private beneficence has identical effect, and again we quote the distinguished statesman:

"In the parish of Southwark, about three hundred and fifty pounds a year, roughly speaking, was given away in doles of bread by charitable people in connection with one of the churches, and, as a consequence of this, the competition for small houses, but more particularly for single-roomed tenements, is, we are told, so great that rents are considerably higher than in the neighbouring district."

Once more we quote from Mr. Churchill:

"Roads are made, streets are made, railway services are improved, electric light turns night into day, electric trams glide swiftly to and fro, water is brought from reservoirs a hundred miles off in the mountains — and all the while the landlord sits still. Every one of these improvements is effected by the labour and cost of other people. Many of the most important are effected at the cost of the municipality and of the ratepayers. To not one of these improvements does the land monopolist, as a land monopolist, contribute, and yet by every one of them the value of his land is sensibly enhanced. He renders no service to the community, he contributes nothing to the general welfare; he contributes nothing even to the process from which his enrichment is derived."

Mr. Churchill then goes on to draw conclusions with which it is hard to disagree: "All goes back to the land, and the landowner, who in many cases — in most cases — is a worthy person utterly unconscious of the character of the methods by which he is enriched, is enabled with resistless strength to absorb to himself a share of almost every public and every private benefit, however important or however pitiful those benefits may be."

Specific operations like these are not the only forces which bring profit to landowners. There are other factors which, acting in the same way, enable "the land monopolist . . . to sit still and watch complacently his property multiplying in value, without either effort or contribution on his part," as Mr. Churchill puts it. These are increases in population and the general progress of all society, both of which contribute to constant enhancement of land values. Therefore, it is needless to deduct from the figures quoted in the subway example the increase of land values that was due to population growth, for this is just as truly a socially created value as is that wrought by the transit system. Glance back at those figures and note how great would be the profit were these included in our totals: the increase in land values was more than two and a half times the cost of the subway.

The Lesson from a "Thruway"

As these pages are being revised we have a striking instance of the increase of land values resulting from the expenditure of public funds. There is agitation for tremendous appropriation for highways, and it is interesting to note how leading real estate operators admit frankly that such a policy will put money into their pockets.

The president of a prominent concern engaged in real estate operations says in substance: "The first to benefit will be real estate. The proof is the astonishing and spectacular rise in values in the few places where adequate highways have already been built. It is happening today in dozens of places over the country. For example, before the East Shore Freeway in California was built, connecting Oakland and San Jose, average raw land values in the area were $500 an acre. Now much of this land has been cut up into industrial subdivisions up to five acres in size. These sell for an average of more than $21,000 an acre. Those closest to the Freeway bring $40,000 an acre."

From this it is easy to see what an enormous amount of money is put into the pockets of real estate speculators through our present tax system. It is true that these operations more particularly affect land beyond city limits, but much of it is in a suburban district which will, or should, be taken into the city before very long. The same principle applies to rural land values, and if the county can raise a large part of its funds by collecting on this enormous profit, which results from the expenditure of taxpayers' money, it will reduce the tax burden on all

the county, including the cities. The same speaker goes on to say:
"Nothing was added to the former marsh and farm land except modern highway facilities. With this additional loan this small section of Alameda County, California, has in seven years attracted more than 29 per cent of all new plants and 43 per cent of the total expenditure for industrial development in the county." This section represents less than 10 per cent of that county, but, "in four years, it accounted for more industrial expansion expenditure than all the rest of the county put together."

The same speaker says, "This example may appear spectacular, but there is nothing new about what roads do to property values. During a twelve-year period residential properties affected by the Bronx River Parkway in New York increased in value by 1178 per cent compared with an increase for areas beyond the parkway of 432 per cent. Similarly properties affected by the Shore Parkway on Long Island increased 76 per cent against a normal average of 19 per cent.

These examples are from the extremes of the country, the East and the West coasts, but the same condition prevails wherever modern highways are built, and the same speaker says that an analysis of more than thirteen hundred parcels of land along the Gulf Freeway in Houston in the five years during construction shows these holdings doubled in value even before the freeway was in full use. He also testifies that the New York State Thruway, of something over five hundred miles, which is just completed as this is written, has had the same effect, and that when plans were announced, immediately a $25,000,000 investment occurred in new plants in Buffalo, and businesses with over $3,000,000 of annual payrolls have developed along the Thruway. In Rochester the Thruway brought 76 new plants, 54 branches of plants and 195 additions and expansions of old plants. In Syracuse new firms employ 17,000 workers with an annual payroll of over $50,000,000, and land that sold at $500 an acre now brings $6,000. The story around Utica, at Albany, and south of Albany is the same, and a new road around Boston attracted some hundred million dollars' worth of new plants to the area.

When an experienced real estate operator recognizes this enormous influence of the expenditure of the taxpayers' money in adding to the values of property of those in his calling, is there any doubt that a wrong is being done in allowing all this gain to go into the hands of a few favored individuals who benefit almost exclusively from what the rest of us pay for? There are plenty of less spectacular illustrations of the same principles, familiar to every motorist. Have you ever noticed how any marked improvement of an old highway always leads to a rash of billboards, filling stations, lunchrooms and "motels"? Clearly, road improvement has added new values to adjacent lands and, since these improvements are paid for by the public, is it not just that the public shall reap at least a part of the benefit?

Another instance comes to mind from personal observation in a southern state. A lawyer, representing a syndicate holding a large tract of land of which the development was being planned, was approached by representatives of those who had to do with the laying out of a thruway. They suggested to the lawyer that the thruway would have an enormous influence on land values and that, if their tract was in a position to benefit by it, the profits of development would be greatly increased. They proposed that the corporation owning these properties make substantial gifts of stock in the corporation to a few favored individuals, whose names these lobbyists promised to produce, and if this was done, they said, those handling this development could dictate pretty much as they pleased just where the road would go through their section of the state.

The lawyer was not inclined to go along with this proposition, whereupon the political representatives pointed out that there was no danger in it of exposure or criticism because no money would change hands and it would involve no interference whatever with the expenditure of state funds. They also said that exactly the same plan had been worked most satisfactorily in another similar development in the same state. In justice to the lawyer, however, who happens to be a personal friend of the writer, we are glad to report that he would have nothing whatever to do with this whole shady transaction; but it goes to show how universally it is recognized that such public improvements increase land values greatly and that political influences are often brought to bear to turn the profits into favored hands.

The Profit of What We Pay for Goes to
Those Who Do Not Even Live in the City

The diversion to private pockets of the revenue earned by the city is bad enough at best, but when this purely local social product goes to alien owners remote from the community, the iniquity is peculiarly irritating. A great building in Indianapolis stands on a leased lot, and ground rents are paid to the owner who lives thousands of miles away and does not contribute to the income which he enjoys even by living in that city. This annual charge, according to the terms of the lease, steadily increases over a long period of years from $16,000 to $35,000, indicating the expectation of unearned profits. The landowner takes no chances, all risk of a decline falling on the tenant. Nor is this all. An initial payment of $100,000 was made by the lessee, and presumably the great building, costing well over half a million dollars, will ultimately revert to the site owner. Can such a procedure be justified by any argument except one of very doubtful ethics — a return on speculation which invloves no quid pro quo other than the privilege of using the land, the gift of the Creator, to which society gives value?

One wonders how the good people of Chicago felt about giving their support to the pro-Nazi activities of Sir Oswald Mosley in England. It is said that funds devoted to the treasonable movement which landed him in prison were derived largely from Chicago ground rents. What reason is there, in common justice, for the people of that city paying tribute to him, to be used in his nefarious purpose? Does not a policy which leads to such results go against the grain of every right-thinking man?

But, to avoid misunderstanding, we repeat that often the landowner suffers acutely, and we have no disposition to blame him for profiting, if he can, by a system which is universally accepted. Besides, despite all that is done for him, he often profits little or not at all. Before entering into these questions, consider the nature of land values and how they differ in character, origin and corollaries from values created by personal effort.

Why Land Has Value

When our forefathers landed on these shores, the whole continent was open to settlement and land could be had anywhere for the taking, for we ignore, as did the pioneers, the rights of the red man. Land had no value and commanded no price, but as soon as the more desirable spots were pre-empted they acquired substantial value in comparison with land in the wilderness, for established settlements made possible companionship, co-operation and some measure of safety. The mere presence of a few neighbors and the simplest of government gave some protection from the Indians and brought advantage.

As population increased and as the better land was appropriated, recourse to the less desirable became necessary. Immediately there was a differential in desirability which found expression in rent and in price, for owners of better land would not part with it without compensation. As time passed and as numbers multiplied, this differential increased, for the free land became less and less desirable, and accordingly rents and prices of the better land advanced. To this there is an important corollary: as rents increase, labor's share of production decreases, and the economist calls labor's share a wage, whether obtained by the direct production of a man working for himself or paid by an employer. We are here dealing with urban land, but why this follows is best illustrated by a simple agricultural example, and the principle is universal and applies to all land.

Suppose a unit of labor produces on the best land five bushels of corn: this constitutes the natural wage of labor, for if land is free it is the reward of the worker for planting and cultivating. But as the best land is taken up and newcomers are forced to be content with poorer land, the same toil produces only four bushels. Their wage is therefore only four, and this is all that any man can earn by his labor, for the owner of better land, if dispossessed of his holding, must take up with the poorer and can produce only four bushels. His extra bushel is the result not of harder or more intelligent labor but of ownership of better land. Land has now acquired value, for it will bring a price at sale or in rent; and, if the first settler had the foresight to take possession of plenty of land, he can live on rents without working, deriving support from values created by the growth and progress of the colony.

But pressure of population is not the only cause of increasing rents, for government plays a part, as in the protection from savages which it affords. As progress comes and as the community provides roads, fire and police protection, water supply, sewers and schools, rents in favored sections advance with each improvement, and land in established communities far outstrips even much better land in the wilderness. Co-operation and collaboration enter into it: increasing population makes possible efficient division of labor, and each settler does not have to be his own blacksmith, spend his time teaching his children, or try to cure his own ills.

Invention, too, must be reckoned with. Without the combination of numbers, the division of labor, and invention, the railroad or the automobile would be impossible, and even so simple a thing as the elevator has enormous effect. Would the site of a great skyscraper be worth what it is if we could do no better than build a "walk-up" of half a dozen floors? For the rural hamlet it does nothing and may even draw off population to the cities. Consider the telephone and telegraph: without them Wall Street would not long remain the financial heart of the continent, and what would happen to its land values?

Value implies monetary worth and the possibility of exchange: it is much the same as price and quite different from usefulness. The air we breathe is a first essential of life, but it has no value. Being limitless, present everywhere and incapable of ownership, it commands no price. So it is with land which may be had for nothing.

Manhattan Island once sold for twenty-four dollars' worth of gimcracks plus a disputed jug of rum, and that land is now worth at least a dozen billions. A few Indians and a handful of Dutchmen have given place to millions and it is the center of life to scores of millions. The people of the island and of the hinterland have created its value. What would it be worth if a scourge wiped out a hundred million of our people or if elevators and subway trains stood still, telephones were silent and electric circuits went dead?

The Lesson from "Made-to-order" Towns

It is not easy to analyze the influences which have created land values in older cities through many years, and better illustration is afforded by towns which, starting recently from scratch, have had a meteoric growth. The land which Gary, Indiana, occupies was, prior to the founding of the city by the steel company, almost worthless and practically uninhabited. Much had been abandoned and sold at tax sales at less than a dollar an acre, although some of it cost the company as much as $800 an acre when plans were noised about and future possibilities became apparent. Twelve years after the steel company moved in, this land was valued at $22,000,000 above its cost, plus all that had been spent on public improvements. In 1908, Mr. Lawson Purdy stated that "this excess value had been created by the large population attracted by these great manufacturing industries. Had the steel company bought all the land in the town of Gary and kept it, it might have conserved the value for itself or for the inhabitants of the town. The value has actually been scattered about: some have profited and some have lost, as many always do when they speculate in vacant land. The town has the reputation of being well managed, but its revenues are inadequate for the public services which would make such a town most attractive. If, today, it enjoyed the revenue represented by the rental value of the land, it would have two and a half times the revenue it actually spends." One wonders what would have been the result had this conservation of rent been coupled with the exemption of building values. Surely it would be a better city with even greater industries and with more residents, and the wise expenditure of the added income would have made possible countless municipal improvements. And these figures take no account of surrounding lands outside the city of which much of the potential value has been lost.

In the town established by the Lackawanna Steel Company, conditions are not as in Gary but they are similar. The excess land value was about $7,000,000 when studied years ago, but since that time population has increased from 16,000 to 30,000 and land values have expanded accordingly. When the town was founded, the population of the present area was about 600, and land which could have been bought in 1899 for about $2,700,000 was assessed seventeen years later — and assessed on a very low basis — at $10,400,000.

For many years Lackawanna had the name of being a dismal

town with "none of the amenities which make town life pleasant" —
no parks, playgrounds or libraries. But it did have some things, including plenty of saloons — 140 of them! — some with great barracks
housing a hundred men, day and night shifts sleeping in the same
beds. It tells its own story in the fact that 60 per cent of the shop
force and 75 per cent of the office force preferred to live in Buffalo
and put up with the expense and annoyance of commuting rather
than live in Lackawanna. Mr. Herbert S. Swan, from whom we have
drawn, concludes with a statement that such industrial towns would
do more to stabilize labor by a solution of the land problem than by
any other policy they might adopt, saying, "There is a right on the
part of the community to enjoy and to benefit by the values which it in
itself creates." Looking at the picture presented by these two industrial
towns, one wonders if even our shrewdest businessmen might not profit
by the study of economics.

These examples are drawn from the past, but they have very real
meaning today, for exactly the same process and mistakes are being
repeated at the great Fairless Works near Morrisville, Pennsylvania, on
the Delaware River. There the U. S. Steel Corporation is developing
a new steel town, offering a splendid opportunity to create from scratch
a model industrial community. Apparently nothing has been learned
from lessons of the past, and doubtless the same old follies will mark
and mar the city which might be a demonstration and example for
all industrial developments.

In such towns as these, the cities might well have acquired all
the land when the city was founded and continued to hold it, leasing
it for ground rent, but in a going city there is no need for purchase,
and titles and tenure should not be disturbed. It is true that title to
land rests on a very different foundation from a claim to that which
has cost us of our time, "the stuff that life is made of," but the buildings
we erect, the orchards we set out, the wells we dig, and all that we
create by our labor belongs to us and, to protect us in their possession,
tenure and title must be respected and these things, themselves, must
be untaxed. What we make we feel instinctively is ours, for it has cost
us of our time and labor: it is the fruit of our natural rights to "life,
liberty and the pursuit of happiness," but claim to land cannot rest
on human production, and this difference has long been recognized.
It was a principle of the Mosaic law that land could not be permanently
alienated, and primitive peoples, governed more by instinctive feelings
than by codes, will seldom sell lands in perpetuity.

Our right to land is the right to share in the common patrimony
of mankind from our Creator. Can anyone maintain that the Almighty
created the earth for the benefit of a few to the exclusion of many?

We hold it in trust and there can be no justification for holding it out of use, to profit by the denial to others of a share in the first essential of life. To have full enjoyment of what we do to and on the land, we must have undisputed tenure, but it is only just that we should make fair compensation for values created by all in that portion of a common birthright held for personal gain and benefit. Lincoln well said: "The land, the earth, God gave to man for his home, sustenance and support . . . An individual, company or enterprise requiring land should have no more than they have in actual use in the management of their legitimate business."

The Wrong Done to Landowners

So much for restoring to the city the values which it creates, but we cannot impose added burdens on the realty owner, who is, by the taxation of his house, already denied the full enjoyment of what is rightfully his. His rehabilitation is quite as vital as is the fianancing of the city, for the city depends on his prosperity. The two problems are essentially one. We create enormous value in land, as shown by the subway example, then we fail to profit, and finally, in the consummation of our folly, we prohibit anyone from profiting.

That much and sometimes all of the value of land is destroyed is evidenced by countless cases of forfeiture rather than payment of tax bills. Driven by a crazy system, we destroy all value in good and useful buildings which are razed to the ground, and then, by unjust and oppressive taxation of new building, we ban future use of the sites, killing even land values. No wonder we groan under our assessments!

How these ruinous processes work is illustrated by an example which finds many parallels. There is one lot a couple of blocks above the state capitol in Albany, well located, with eighty-foot frontage on two good residential streets. It was formerly occupied by the houses of prominent families, one with an extensive garden. Some years ago it was sold for redevelopment. Pending drawing of plans and arranging of financing, the first step was to tear down existing houses, to cut tax bills. This meant a double loss: the value of the houses to the new owners was wiped out and tax receipts to the city were cut, and that was that.

Plans were drawn for buildings in keeping with present-day needs, but study showed that they would be in much the same predicament as the houses razed: taxes would absorb so large a part of earnings that little or nothing would be left. Things dragged along for years, with revision of plans and re-examination of the problem; there were changes of ownership, but nothing was done, for the dilemma was unconquerable. The lot might remain vacant, bringing in nothing but tax bills—the assessment was $48,000 and the taxes about $1,700—or it might be built upon and yield a substantial return which would be gobbled up by the tax collector. For some years taxes were paid, but finally the owners, tiring of sending good money after bad and unable to find a purchaser, gave up. After many trials and tribulations and serious losses to successive owners, the property was finally acquired as a site for a building to be occupied by a state department—an unfortunate departure from the type of buildings of the neighborhood. Presumably the site was bought at a tax-sale price and the state was apparently the only tenant prepared to pay a "rent" which makes the deal profitable.

This may be an extreme case, but there are plenty like it and the process goes on day after day, in varying degrees, the country over. Regardless of what assessment books say, the value of land is sharply reduced and often wiped out by a prohibitive tax on buildings without which most city lots can earn little. Here in lies the explanation of the universal howl against assessments: by a prohibitive tax on buildings we so reduce the value which would otherwise attach to sites that assessments are out of line and become the source of complaint.

More will be said about tax assessments and the necessity for drastic revision of present practices, and here we call attention to only a few glaring evils. In some cities realty often sells at prices far below assessment figures. Some years ago the sale of a large holding in New York City was reported at less than a tenth of its valuation, and we noted an advertisement of a well-located house offered at a quarter of the assessment. Today land assessments are practically always far below the values which would attach to city land *if tax conditions made it profitable to build*, and yet, at the same time, they are often far in excess of current sales prices, depressed and sometimes wiped out, as shown by forfeiture under a mad tax system. It is true that in recent years there has been a marked recovery in many cites, but inflated realty prices do nothing to help those ruined during depression days.

A Simple Remedy

For this double wrong—loss to city and injury to realty owners—there is a simple remedy:

Transfer the tax load from building to land values. This will restore to owners what is justly theirs, enabling many to derive a profit from holdings not even earning tax costs today, and it will increase site values—not sales prices, but true value measured in earning capacity.

This transfer of taxation, if we so like to call it, actually means the ending of taxation, for collection of a just ground rent by the city for values and benefits it gives is no more taxation than is its collection by a landlord. In dictionary words, taxation is "a compulsory contribution for the support of government," and a just rent cannot be so described no matter to whom it is paid. It is payment for values received in public improvements, services and progress of government and of society, and it should obviously go to those who create these values.

Such change will involve legislation and some readjustments, but if made progressively over a number of years, reducing the tax on buildings and increasing ground rents each year until the change is complete, it will not be difficult. The method is worked out and a formula offered, but first a word about some broad general principles. How land and labor values differ.

Differences between land values and those produced by labor are many and far-reaching. Land is the gift of the Creator and not the product of human toil. It is rigidly fixed and limited; but crops, houses, gadgets and what not can be produced until the end of time, if there is free access to land and its resources and willingness to labor. Land is sometimes almost an abstract thing, with its value lying not in intrinsic physical properties but in mere space and location. These are fixed, unlike things which man can produce and move about. True, the Empire State Building cannot be moved bodily to western prairies, but its mate could be erected there, and the value of the location is an attribute of *site* and not of building. A hydroelectric plant must be built where there is water power; but, again, its peculiar value is of *site* and not of iron and concrete. Even when we "make" land we must have site and space, and values represented by filling, draining, and grading are as truly labor values as those of building, and entirely apart from land values.

Each tract of land is unique and cannot possibly be duplicated. There are four corners of Main and Market streets but only four, and they lie on different sides of the street and differ in exposure and desirability. Your ownership of a knife does not preclude my owning its mate, but the land you own I can never duplicate in every detail. For these reasons land is capable of monopoly in a way impossible in the case of most commodities.

The price of ordinary commodities is determined by supply and demand. When the latter exceeds the former, prices rise and increased supply, stimulated by unfilled demand, brings about a balance, but if supply is excessive, production halts until the surplus is exhausted and price again spurs production. To insure supply, price must cover all production costs or output will cease, and taxes are as integral a part of costs as is what is paid for material, power or labor. With the supply of land fixed by our inability to produce it, demand is the only variable and alone determines price. The price of land, whether at sale or in rent, is fixed by competition in the market and is influenced by monopoly of ownership and not by any production costs.

The Assessment of Land Values

Our philosophy of land assessment is fallacious. Established on the basis of sales price, it takes into account only values which can be sold or transferred, ignoring entirely values lodged in government and represented by taxing powers, undisputed, exercised remorselessly always and everywhere, and taking priority over all other claims.

This supreme claim of the state to land is and always has been universally recognized by all legal authorities, and it is frankly asserted in many of our state constitutions, as in that of New York, which declares: "The people in their right of sovereignty are deemed to possess the original and ultimate property in and to all lands within the jurisdiction of the state." In monarchies the final title lies in the Crown, and this principle was at the foundation of the feudal system and, by delegation, underlay the old manorial system of the Hudson Valley. Indeed, if we trace our titles back, we shall find that they are generally based on grants and charters of European kings or on patents from our own governments, colonial, state, or national. The right of "eminent domain" — the right of government or its delegated agent to take any land for public use, paying for it not the price set by its owner but as fixed by a court — is another reminder of the supreme right of the people.

This division of ownership can be readily worked out in figures. We take as an example a city where the tax rate and prevailing interest rates are approximately equal — about 4½ per cent. If the holder of a piece of land pays $900 a year for tenure, the property is worth $20,000, arrived at by capitalizing gross income at the prevailing rate of interest. However, though this amount is paid by the tenant, one half must be turned over to the tax collector, so actual ownership is divided equally between city and titleholder, each deriving an income of $450. Capitalizing the net income enjoyed by the titleholder puts his value in the land at $10,000, and that is what it is normally assessed at, but *this figure represents only the value which the titleholder can sell.* Accustomed to thinking in terms of sales price and market value, we mistake this for the full value, ignoring the equity of the taxing authority.

The proportionate shares of ownership by the city and by the titleholder depend upon the ratio of taxes to net return to the owner. In our example there is an equal division, but should the tax rate go to 6 per cent, the city would get $600 and the owner only $300, so two thirds of the value would be lodged in the city and only one third would remain with the titleholder. Should the tax go to 9 per cent, all the value would be taken by the city: no equity would be left to the owner and the value of the title would theoretically shrink to zero, although the tenant still pays $900 a year. *What the tenant pays is the true index of real value; and, though the equity of the titleholder would disappear and sales value be wiped out, the lot would nevertheless be worth just as much as before, but the value would all be vested in the city.* This illustrates the universal fallacy in assessing land values: we mistakenly assess in utter disregard of values lodged in the government, basing assessment only on the value held by the titleholder, because this is all that he can sell and so it becomes the gauge of the market price.

This is a very practical point when it comes to questions of levying a higher tax on land. It is difficult today to work out a basis for levying such a tax because, as we increase the tax, the value *as we assess it* continually shrinks, but if we assess all land *at its true value*, we shall have a just basis for taxation and this difficulty disappears. It would be no departure from our general practice in taxing other things: the income tax is levied on income and not on what is left of income after paying the tax. We should base taxation on the rental which land will command — the amount which the tenant is willing to pay — regardless of whether it goes to the city in taxes or is divided with the titleholder. This division of the ownership of land is something very real and not a mere theoretical abstraction, for the exactions of the tax collector frequently lead to tax sales and forfeiture. *The wrong done to the realty owner lies not in site-value taxation but in seizure of what is justly our own personal property*, through taxation of buildings and improvements, which are the fruit of personal life and labor.

If we prefer we could simply assess ground rent and take that — or most of it — for the support of government, but it may be well to compute a capitalized valuation for purposes other than local taxation. In some states it is important as a limit on bonded indebtedness: it may affect distribution of state funds, and it is sometimes the basis of state taxation. To compute this capitalized value, the full ground rent should be capitalized at the current tax rate, because this is the rate of return to the city. It is often asked how ground rents will be computed in the absence of sales price: the answer is that the capitalized value of land, as we see it today, is figured from rent and not the other way around. There is not the slightest necessity of going in circles, first computing capitalization from rent and then rent from capitalization. Think in terms of ground rent — what use and and occupancy are worth — and avoid this roundabout circumlocution.

The matter of reforming the methods of assessment of land values calls for study and must be approached with regard to existing laws and constitutional controls.

Our first aim should be to correct the often flagrant disregard of law today: for example; in many communities not the slightest regard is paid to the common legal requirement that all assessments must be at "full value." Where laws or constitutions embody such requirements, we find sometimes that, by common consent or by local ordinances, assessments are limited to a mere fraction of true values. We think of one western city where all improvements are assessed at 50 per cent of true values and sites at only 25 per cent. Frequently assessments in different cities are so out of line that the state must step in with equalization figures to correct manifest discrepancies.

Every effort should be made to correct these evils and to bring assessments closer to true values. They are today falsely computed because cognizance is taken only of that portion of the value which is vested in the titleholder.

Then, if possible, every effort should be made to establish legally assessments at the true figures, based on the economic rent which land will command and not on only that portion of that rent which goes to the titleholder, ignoring the equity held by the taxing authorities. Assessments should be based not on sales but on ground rent, and that includes not only what the titleholder collects but what the city collects in taxes.

Even doing this, there may still be a problem in collecting what the landholder should pay, and must pay, if we are to cease confiscating the purely personal values by taxing the improvements made by individual effort. It might not be easy to increase land assessments to a full and just figure or to increase the tax rates on sites, because frequently there are statutory limits on tax rates. The difficulty of a limitation on tax rates might perhaps be overcome by a simultaneous reduction of the taxes on improvements. It might be possible to substitute for present laws, setting an arbitrary limit on tax rates, legislation removing these restrictions as applied to sites but setting far more drastic restrictions, and ultimately the complete removal of taxes on improvements.

We believe that there is a real and an almost automatic factor which will greatly facilitate the sounder assessment and taxing of realty. We refer to the very positive influence of improvement taxation on land values and repeat once more that any tax on realty *uses* will be automatically reflected in lower values on land, for the value of land depends upon the profit which may be obtained by using it, or by producing from it. Therefore all interference with profitable use, by prohibiting building upon it, will result in a marked, and sometimes a ruinous, decrease in land values. So often is this condition seen that frequently land is forfeited for nonpayment of taxes. The owner finds that profitable use of land is virtually prohibited and that therefore the land is valueless to him. Conversely, freeing the improvement of land will manifestly increase its value.

This appears to be borne out by the Cowan studies of land values in Australia and the effect on those values of exempting improvements. It is apparent, too, in many situations at home. We have in mind a piece of property where the site is assessed at $15,000 and the house, an obsolete one, at $7,000. This lot, in the opinion of one who should know, would have justified a million-dollar-apartment-house development had it not been for improvement taxation, for the tax on a million-dollar building would be about $45,000 today. This high overhead settled the question once and for all, and so the lot continues to be occupied by the old, obsolete house of little value and the property has greatly declined and is hardly earning its tax bill.

Suppose we trebled the present tax on the site, increasing it from $675 a year to about $2,000, but eliminated the $45,000 tax bill which the million-dollar apartment house would have to pay. The city would gain, collecting three times as much in taxes as it does today, but, unless there is a drastic change in tax policy, no improvement will be made and no contribution to the acute housing needs of the city. The return to the owner would be increased by about $43,000, and the return earned by the entire property would be increased by about $40,000 over what it would be under today's system. If money is worth 5 per cent, this increase of $43,000 in the earnings of this property would represent an increased capital value of nearly $800,000 and, since the value of a building never goes above replacement cost, this increase would attach to the site value. Is it not obvious that such a change in our tax system would add tremendously to the value of many pieces of land?

We mention speculative lots assessed at $400 each. Obviously even this low assessment is beyond their present value, for the owner prefers to forfeit the lots rather than pay the tax. We believe that these lots, with the housing situation as it is today and the present high cost of building, would justify houses costing at least $20,000. Today these would be taxed about $900 each year; but, under our proposed plan, trebling the tax on land values would make it possible to eliminate all taxes on improvements. Suppose, to play it safe, instead of trebling these taxes we multiply them by four, raising the tax of about $16 a year to about $64 a year. The owners would then find it possible to build $20,000 untaxed houses and the tax on the site would be relatively insignificant. They would save the $900 tax which would today be levied on the house. Of course the city would gain greatly.

It may not be easy for the reader to whom these ideas are new to see this at first glance, but the writer has been studying these questions for a quarter of a century or more; as a landowner, and as one who has had some experience in real estate operation, he is convinced that the change which we propose would accomplish three important objectives. It would stabilize and strengthen city finance, it would benefit greatly the real estate operator who is doing something for the ctiy, and it would go far toward clearing up the housing problem and toward eliminating the problem of slums. We believe that every class would gain by it with the single exception of the dog-in-the-manger speculator — the miser who buys land and holds onto it, doing nothing with it but simply seeking to glean where others sow. True, he is often disappointed in these hopes, but nevertheless the harm is done.

Any basic change in assessment methods may call for legislation, but to secure this should not be too difficult. Assessments in themselves mean little unless taken in conjunction with tax rates. In some cities speculative interests have succeeded in limiting land assessments to 25 percent of the partial value lodged in the titleholder, and it should not be hard to get this palpable undervaluation corrected and then, by a little education, particularly of the landless and the younger generation, to get a sounder system established, assessing not only the fragmentary portion of the titleholder but also the greater equity of the taxing authority, and this would be greatly facilitated by simultaneous reduction of the tax on improvements.

There is another side light on land valuations. Years ago it was found that total assessments of land values in a city may generally be roughly approximated by multiplying $1,000 by the population of the city. This is of course only approximate and gives only sales value of the land and not the true value, for it ignores the values already lodged in the city. Checking land values as assessed in many cities on this basis shows that generally they are much undervalued and, unquestionably in view of today's inflation and the reduced value of our money, we should multiply by at least $1,500 instead of by $1,000.

To get any scientifically correct appraisal of land values today is difficult at best, and to express a general opinion is hazardous, for conditions vary tremendously. As we say, in one state they are systematically underassessed at 25 per cent of a low valuation, and yet in some cities land assessments are sometimes excessive. Often the site values of old buildings are underassessed, but in the case of new construction there is apparently a feeling that assessments should be in harmony with the cost of buildings and therefore sometimes sites are overassessed.

We have talked with Mr. Allan J. Wilson of St. Petersburg, Florida, who has made a study of these questions on a wide area, and we believe it is safe to say that assessments of land values are often at about 10 per cent of sales value. In checking this report with the opinion of others, including real estate operators with wide experience, there seems to be a rather surprising agreement with this 10 per cent estimate. We believe that it is perfectly safe to say that were improvements and franchises relieved from all taxation there would not be the slightest hardship to the titleholder in multiplying the site assessments by five, and often by ten, and we believe that this general increase might be effected without much difficulty, were there some degree of education of the general public.

It is well in advocating such a change to stress the points which will generally win favor rather than the points which may arouse controversy. Emphasize the rapid reduction of the taxation of improvements, the incentive which it will give to building and the stimulus it will give to industry. Then point out that the only way that this can be effected it by increasing the tax on land values, which will have no unfortunate effect but which on the contrary will do away with the inflation of land prices and reckless speculation.

The same argument may often be phrased in different terms, making quite a different impression, and all in perfect honesty and without deceit. We are reminded of the story of two monks, both of them confirmed smokers, who were required to spend an hour a day in meditation. They agreed to ask the Superior if it was permissible to smoke while meditating and then get together and compare notes. One reported the Superior as saying yes, it was quite all right. The other said that he met with an emphatic no. The first had asked if it was all right to meditate while smoking, and the other had asked if there was any objection to smoking while meditating.

Present-day taxation is the betrayal of our professed belief in the natural rights of "life, liberty and the pursuit of happiness" and can be justified only in times of dire extremity, when even the sacrifice of life is demanded for common defense. Property rights should be respected, whether communal in values given by all society by our common heritage from the Creator, or personal in the product of individual life and labor. The collection of ground rent, to be returned

[28]

to all through the services of that great co-operative enterprise which we call government, is the only way by which we can end the twin evils of the appropriation by landholders of the rent which belongs to all, and the robbery of the landholders, depriving them of the full benefit of what they do to and on land. They will profit more by this freedom to use land than they will lose through the collection of ground rent by the city to which it justly belongs.

Our problem then is to work out a method of making this change-over while supporting government and protecting the individual, now defrauded of the earnings of his life and labor. This means the collection of ground rent instead of taxes on improvements. To accomplish this we should, by appropriate legislation, (1) steadily decrease the taxes on buildings and comparable improvements until wholly eliminated, and (2) increase all land assessments to their full value, collecting a constantly increasing proportion, and finally practically all of the ground rent for the support of government.

Some Contrasts and Benefits

All of man's needs — his food, clothing, shelter, and all that makes life possible or worth living — must come, in last analysis, from the land, if we include in that word all the resources of the world about us. To make what nature offers available and useful, labor is always necessary, for we must discover, extract, produce, fabricate and transport the raw materials if they are to serve us. Therefore, whatever is taken to support government must be obtained by levies on either land, the source, or labor, the means of production.

This argument may appear too materialistic, ignoring the greater things of life, but here we deal only with the material and not with the metaphysical. If man is to be anything more than a brute, he must have the things of the spirit — vision, conscience, companionship and aspirations — but even these are dependent upon physical existence. The child cannot have the full measure of a mother's love and care unless both have the physical necessities of life. If it be said that we make too much of property rights, remember that property has no rights whatever. Your shoes have no right to walk the pavement unless you are in them, and your car has no right on the highway although you have a right to drive it there. What we call property rights are always personal — the right of the person and not of the thing — and any attempt to distinguish between what we thoughtlessly call property rights and personal rights leads only to confusion.

Government must be supported either by a charge against the value given land by our common life or by taxes on the use of land by labor. The landowner cannot escape: he must pay either on the share of our common heritage which he holds or on the use to which he puts it. There is no alternative. *The only way in which the right to what labor yields can be fully respected is by levying a charge for values and services which society gives to the land he calls his.* In land values, or ground rents, we have an automatic index to what society does for him. We must therefore choose between collecting ground rent for the support of government or taxing labor values. In one case we give advantage to idleness and speculation; in the other we give incentive to the production of men's needs. No matter how heavily we tax the land, we cannot reduce our resources one iota, but rather we give stimulus to production. If land must carry a heavy overhead, it becomes increasingly imperative to use it productively, *but taxing what labor puts into or takes out of the land reduces the profit of labor and the incentive to production, keeping all mankind the poorer.*

To contrast the effects of taxation, take a simple illustration. What relation has the value of a rare postage stamp or a treasured autograph to the cost of paper and ink? Most of us could spend our days signing our names on the finest paper and with the costliest ink, but the materials would only be wasted, whereas the rough scrawls made by other men on the cheapest paper are sometimes worth thousands of dollars. The values lies in something not measured in production costs. When we buy a Rembrandt, do we buy canvas and paint? Contrast the effect of taxing books published today with the taxing of rare first editions. Every tax which enters into the cost of publishing this little book, every tax all along the line from the time the trees are cut to make the paper and ores mined to make type and machinery will — we hope! — be covered in what you pay for it, for if the publisher cannot recover his outlay he will soon be out of business. Every tax on every element increases price, restricts markets and, finally, means fewer books.

A tax on an irreplaceable item such as a rare book has an effect diametrically opposite. It depresses price instead of raising it, for were the ownership of such books heavily penalized by taxation, they would be far less coveted. Make the tax high enough and few could afford to own them and such volumes would soon find their way to junk piles or to tax-exempt libraries. With land it is precisely the same as with other irreplaceables: taxation decreases price and, if high enough, would destroy all sales value. Few would wish to own land just for the sake of owning it, and land speculation would end. We would seek only as much as could be put to profitable use, and use-value would be greatly increased were buildings untaxed. Man is absolutely dependent upon land and we can never tax it out of use. Rather, we can tax it into use.

The Effect on "Rents"

What we call rent is usually made up of two very different components: true rent for the site, and an item, more accurately interest, for the use of the building and, perhaps, its contents. This is clear if we hire a lot on long-term lease and build with borrowed money, and many of our greatest buildings are erected on that plan. Then we pay rent for the site and interest on a mortgage covering building value, but the latter is no more true rent than is payment for the use of a rowboat or a typewriter.

It is only with the tax on buildings that the tenant is concerned, for it is this tax, and this tax only, which adds to his "rent" bill. As we have seen, what is paid for the use of the site will be unchanged whether collected by city, by landlord, or by the two jointly. True rent we must always have as long as sites differ in desirabiilty, for rent is only the expression of this differential. Taxes on a building are passed on and re-collected from the tenant. A tax on the site, if we like so to call it, comes positively and finally out of the pocket of the owner, and he will be more than compensated by opportunity to use this lot profitably without added tax penalty. Therefore, the collection of true rent by the city will not increase by one penny what the tenant pays, while the elimination of the tax on buildings will be a definite saving.

If money is worth 6 per cent and the tax rate is 3 per cent, a house costs 9 per cent a year, and on this basis the tenant must pay, and the cost to owner-occupant must be figured in the same way. Were the house untaxed, the "rent" of *the house* could be reduced by a third and, as we have seen, the increased levy on the site cannot be passed on to the tenant. The owner would still net 6 per cent *on the house*, which is all he clears on it today. With this reduction in "rent," he could fill premises perhaps now vacant. This saving would solve the housing problem, for its crux lies in the fact that, with rents so inflated, tenants cannot afford to pay enough to make it profitable to build. Reduce costs by the elimination of the tax on houses, and many who now live in slums will be able to afford decent quarters. Such a saving would mean much to many and there would be a livelier and more profitable demand for decent houses. To the frequent but not very bright comment that it matters little how we assess the tax if the amount remains unchanged, the answer is that it makes all the difference in the world. Taxes may increase "rents" and discourage building, or they may have exactly the opposite effect, reducing "rents" and giving incentive to new construction. No matter how we tax the site, untaxing the houses will make building more profitable and give

[31]

incentive to those who contribute to meeting housing needs.

It may be well to enlarge on this argument, for it is frequently misunderstood and misrepresented. If building and site values are equal for a city as a whole, to exempt the former will necessitate doubling the levy on the latter. What difference does it make if the tax be figured at $500 on the house and $500 on the lot or if the entire $1,000 be assessed on the latter alone? The "how" of taxation is quite as important as the "how much," for under the change the building becomes far more profitable and the mere holding of land matters but little. Surely the owner will be far less inclined to tear down the building if demolition will not cut the tax bill, and many a house will be preserved. Leave things as they are and many an old but serviceable house will be razed for no other reason than to cut the tax bill. Surely the owner of a vacant lot or an obsolete tenement will be more disposed to build if by so doing he incurs no added levy. We shall have more and better housing at lower "rentals," and speculative land, now held idle, will be built upon with profit to all.

The effect on mortgages is self-evident. Most urban mortgages are on properties which are improved or about to be improved. Taxes generally have priority over all other claims and must be paid before interest, so even what we call a first mortgage is actually a secondary obligation. Wiping out the tax on the building will increase the margin of safety of all subsequent obligations, and loans will be negotiated with greater ease and security and at a lower rate.

In one city a great building has bonds outstanding and in default, aggregating about $1,000,000. The property is assessed at $1,750,000 and the tax bill is $52,500, of which $37,500 is levied on the building. Under the proposed plan, it would pay about $30,000 in ground rents and enough would be saved to cover half the interest on the 4½ per cent bonds. This saving, coupled with earnings, would meet interest charges. The whole situation would be stabilized, with tax payments assured; but, if conditions are unchanged, this property will sooner or later be lost, bringing disaster to all.

Speculation and Its Evils

In a growing city, land values tend normally to rise and outlying sections, which give promise of early development, are snapped up by speculators, sometimes to be held for many years. Beyond this belt lies a remote section which shows little speculative advance, and to it many must resort to procure homes within their means, suffering all the drawbacks and expense of time-consuming transportation. Thus we have a congested core with prices correspondingly inflated, surrounded by a speculative zone where little or no development is taking place. Beyond that belt there is a semi-suburban tract fast being taken up but, in the intermediate area, neglected and deserted, everything is held up pending the realization of speculative hopes and, though these are often doomed to disappointment, the harm is done. There are tropical plants which send out growth in all directions while the parent plant dies off, and many a city presents a comparable picture. The city itself decays and areas are all but abandoned; outlying sections, beyond city limits and contributing nothing to its finances, thrive and flourish, while the city faces a constantly shrinking tax base. A wiser policy would give us better planned cities with land values more uniform and normal. The tax on a $10,000 house on a lot of equal value is half against the house; but, were the house untaxed, its cost would be no factor in the tax bill and there would be every inducement to spend $19,000 on the house and only $1,000 on the lot. Taxes would then be paid on an assessment of $1,000 instead of $20,000 and cheaper sites in less congested neighborhoods would be sought, providing better housing and a better-balanced development of the city.

Such idle speculative areas are most wasteful, necessitating extension of the services of the city and the utilities through profitless belts to serve outlying districts. In Los Angeles County, for instance, there were, for some years, water mains, sewers, paving and sidewalks for twice the present number of houses, and the upkeep cost of these almost useless things was estimated at $3,000,000 a year. The Municipal Finance Officers Association declares that "the most fundamental requirement for stabilizing real estate values, and therefore municipal revenues, is the control of land use and prevention of blighted areas," and surely great tracts of vacant land entailing heavy and profitless expenditure are as blighted areas as can be found.

The waste from the wild speculation in Florida land of some years ago was everywhere apparent, and the statement that civic improvements always benefit landowners requires qualification, for unwise and untimely public expenditure profits nobody. Great stretches around existing towns were laid out by the overhopeful: lots surveyed, streets paved, water mains and sewers laid and even street lighting provided. When the bubble burst, all was abandoned: grass grew in the streets, sidewalks became overgrown and poles lay in the gutters. Even when speculation does not blow up completely there is terrific waste from premature development, and the profit, when there is a profit, often goes to outsiders who contribute little or nothing, only gambling on what other men do. "To foment a good-sized boom requires the invasion of both men and money from other places," as witness the wild Florida bubble which drew both profiteers and victims from all over the country.

The extent to which speculation in urban land often goes is seldom realized, nor do we appreciate the evils it brings. As Mr. Harold S. Buttenheim, long the editor of *The American City*, says, "Bitter experience is demonstrating that the great American game, land gambling, instead of being an innocent venture or a speculation of concern only to private individuals who play the game, is too often a public tragedy with most of the losses underwritten by the taxpaying public. How to regulate land speculation with justice to legitimate and socially ueseful business interests is one of the most important and difficult of civic problems." The simple and direct way is to frame our policies so that enterprise will be encouraged and speculation checked.

Some speculation offers a peculiar problem. We cite as an example a case which may not look like speculation but bears all the earmarks, for the owner persists in holding an inadequately used property in the forlorn hope that it will come back in value by reason of improvements made and paid for by the taxpayers and the growth of the city.

In a downtown section of a great city there is a building erected seventy years ago to house a business, long since reorganized and removed to a modern building in better location. The old building passed to a son, an invalid, whose personal income exceeds his business capacity. He would be as surprised to meet a new idea as to encounter an ichthyosaurus, and sees no reason why the old building, unsuited to the times, neglected, disintegrating, constantly attracting a less and less desirable class of tenants, does not earn the return it once did.

The owner might be forced to sell, were the tax on the site to be almost trebled. He would doubtless feel abused and yet he would be better off. Insurance, upkeep and depreciation today take a heavy toll, and he is indisposed to spend a penny to modernize the property, and indeed, with improvements heavily taxed as they are today, it would be a doubtful investment. Under a sensible tax plan, the property would still have broad possibilities and would probably be readily sold.

Speculation discourages the would-be homeowner. The hope of speculative profits arising from increase of site values often deters an owner from selling at a reasonable price to one who would gladly build or purchase a home, for the landlord capitalizes his hopes and asks a proportionately higher price. Were the city to collect full ground rent, there would be no increment to the landowner and there would be every reason for selling and the tenant's buying or building an untaxed house. The city would tend to become one of homeowners, to be desired on every count, for those with a stake in the community enjoy the satisfaction and security of ownership and make a far better citizenry.

Examples of Our Folly

Obviously there will be greater incentive to build if the builder receive all the profit from his investment than if the tax collector take it in part or in whole, but this is only a portion of the story. Reconstruction, renovation and even decent maintenance bring higher tax bills. Apparently some cities prefer to look shabby and to disintegrate, for even the painting of a house frequently means a tax penalty and material improvement is heavily taxed. In a large and thriving village a well-to-do retired farmer lived at the intersection of the two main highways. He was active in affairs connected with agriculture and neglected his place. Shabby and run-down, it needed repairs and paint; the lawns were a disgrace. Finally he pulled himself together, rebuilt his porches, painted his house, resodded the lawns and did some excellent ornamental planting. The whole town presented a different aspect, by reason of his conspicuous location — but his tax bill was so increased that he declared that never again would he spend an unnecessary penny on improvements. There was no more work for artisans and gardeners and all the town suffered.

Such instances can be multiplied indefinitely. An acquaintance of the writer found his tax bill jumped when he built a simple sleeping porch for an invalid son. In one town the assessors snooped around and raised assessments of every house which had been insulated — and this at a time when fuel was strictly rationed! Is there any earthly reason why such sensible, employment-giving operations should be penalized? They stimulate business; they save needed fuel; they make life easier and healthier. For such policies there is neither argument of justice nor excuse on a shabby plea of expediency. In other lands, chimneys and windows were once taxed, and consequently houses were smoky, dark and ill-ventilated. We see the folly of it now, but is it any wiser to tax insulation and sleeping porches, making our people suffer from cold of winter and the heat of summer? If it is folly to tax windows and chimneys, how about roofs, floors and walls? We tax not only windows and chimneys but the whole house!

In a city where there was taxation of personal property — that unsavory combination of guesswork and perjury — a substantial businessman who by mere luck had escaped personal taxation built an $18,000 house. It was assessed at $20,000 and on it he paid a tax of about $800, but the assessors were not content. On the undeniable assumption that if he could build such a residence he probably had at least $10,000 salted away, he was taxed on another $400, so actually the building of the house cost him $1,200 in taxes each year. His business flourished and outgrew its hired quarters. Because he was unable to find a suitable building, preliminary investigation was made of the wisdom of building to house his enterprise. Mindful of past experience, he moved slowly, knowing full well that a $500,000 building would be taxed over $20,000 a year and that his personal property assessment would be doubled or perhaps multiplied several times. While weighing the pros and cons, he received a good offer for his business and sold. It was moved to another city, some employees moving with it while others were out of jobs, and the city lost a long-established business as the result of a crazy tax system.

The Benefits of Greater Wisdom

An immediate effect of the transfer of taxation would be to halt the demolition of good and serviceable buildings, to spur new construction, and to encourage the modernizing of old buildings. Slums and firetraps would give way to new housing, and one problem would be on the way to solution, with profit and without subsidy. The aspect of many sections would be changed and there would be a stabilizing of city revenues, with substantial economies, for sociologists tell us that decent housing means real savings in relief and in police, fire and health departments. In New York City the incidence of tuberculosis, diphtheria and meningitis is more than twice as high in "old-law" tenements as in "new-law"; and in Philadelphia the death rate from such diseases in some districts is five times that in others. Boston shows striking variations in infant mortality, and the same contrasts are evident wherever studied. Crime, too, is related to housing, as is also juvenile delinquency. We grant that cause and effect are not always readily unscrambled, and which produces which is like the question of the hen and the egg; but there is no question whatever that slum housing is a direct and very costly cause of many evils.

Some Recent Experiences

That such results would follow from slum clearance and from better housing is self-evident, but confidence is strengthened by experience. We have drawn on many sources and a recent article by Donald Robinson in the *National Municipal Review* confirms what we have said.

Experience in many cities and in many states demonstrates beyond question that slum clearance and better housing, while of benefit to the poor and ill-housed, bring benefits to practically everyone. These secondary results of slum clearance and decent housing — and the two

[36]

generally go together — are sometimes quite as important as the direct benefits to those who are housed.

Even if we discount the statistics of the Public Housing Administration, as perhaps slanted to support their work, these figures nevertheless prove much. Slum districts often account for about half of our major crimes and for more than half of the juvenile delinquency and frequently for almost as large a proportion of the communicable diseases. Thirty-five per cent of the fires in some cities are in slum districts. In a New Jersey city the incidence of tuberculosis in the slums was twice that in better districts, and of other communicable diseases the rate was about one third less in the better sections. Thousands of dollars were saved by the rehabilitation of slum districts, in visiting nurses, hospital and ambulance costs. In Baltimore rehabilitation brought a cut of nearly 50 per cent in the tuberculosis rate.

In Cleveland the juvenile delinquency rate in new housing is reported to be about one half of what it is in slum areas, and in Philadelphia the rate of juvenile arrests in fifteen new housing projects was a trifle over 2 per cent, but in the slum areas where most of the public-housing children formerly lived the rate ranged as high as 11½ per cent. In the same city the number of arrests were reduced to less than one fifth of what it had been.

It is interesting to note some incidental improvements following slum clearance. In Newark slum eradication worked a marked improvement in school records: attendance better by 7 per cent, academic grades by 10 per cent, and in various intangible ratings, such as personality, habits, etc., the improvement ranged sometimes as high as 20 per cent. Formerly in Savannah about 19 per cent of the crime originated in the slum districts; since clearance, less than 1 per cent is traced to this area, and in Norfolk, Virginia, the police report that districts where no one was safe at night are now safe for anyone. In fire hazard there is also a marked change. In Newark there were four times as many fires in slum districts as in modern housing projects and the cost of fire protection has been cut to about a quarter of what it formerly was and naturally there is a corresponding saving in human life. Fires in slum areas in New York once cost about sixty lives a year, but not a single life has been lost in the new housing. Fatal home accidents are also similarly reduced.

There are interesting side lights in the effect of decent living on family life and on the habits of the people. In North Carolina about a third of the whites and about half of the Negro families who left public housing developments moved because they had purchased homes of their own, and in Louisville considerably more than half who moved from low-rent projects moved into newly purchased homes.

[37]

As might be expected and has been shown many times, these improved conditions have brought real economy in city financing. The slums of Atlanta consumed about 53 per cent of the city income and paid only 6 per cent of the real estate tax. In Baltimore every acre of slums showed a deficit of $2,500 each year for the city government to meet. All these figures are a real argument for the change which we advocate, to eradicate slums and to better housing. There is considerable statistical evidence to prove the point that we have made, that these improvements will react upon surrounding districts to increase land values and thus, under the system which we advocate, to increase city revenues.

In a thirty-block district of Brooklyn the total assessed valuation of buildings of the area surrounding the public health project shows assessed valuations increased by 50 per cent, which is twice the rate for Brooklyn property as a whole. In Stuyvesant Town, the slum-clearance project financed by the Metropolitan Life in the Borough of Manhattan, valuations of a thirty-two-block area in the neighborhood increased about 68 per cent, and on one three-block stretch the increase was nearly 200 per cent.

This clearly shows that the program advocated would not be as difficult to finance as might be at first supposed. Surely where the improvements *made by other people in other properties* increase valuations of adjoining property, which contributed nothing, by 200 per cent, there is no reason for not taking a large part of this increased ground rent. In Pittsburgh a sixty-acre slum area was cleaned up, about one half of it being turned into a park and therefore taken off the tax rolls, while the other half was used for a new housing project. Land values in the rehabilitated district increased by over ten million dollars, and the Pennsylvania Economy League says that "the re-development program has affected the entire city and it is estimated that the over-all gain during the first five years was thirty-five million dollars in valuations."

Is not this pretty conclusive evidence that the change would not be difficult to make? In Greater New York, where finances are very much of a problem, it is conservatively estimated that taxes from land alone, the worth of which has been boosted because the properties adjoin slum-clearance projects, amount to over two million dollars.

In Murfreesboro, Tennessee, a small city that formerly collected about $2,000 a year in taxes on slum areas, they collect today ten times as much, and Perth Amboy, N. J. has seen the tax receipts raised from about $23,000 to a $170,000 by re-development of slums. We believe that the figures for these last two cities should be revised, for apparently they include improvement values as well as land values.

[38]

However, this would clearly react on all surrounding land where there is not necessarily any improvement, and it is quite probable that in these cities, had improvements been exempted, there would have been a still more striking increase of the assessments on land, for there would have been, in all probability, a great extension of the improved areas.

These studies and many others indicate clearly that there would be three results from the program which we recommend. First, it would settle once and for all the problems of slums and housing. Second, it would offset a great part of the reduction in tax receipts that results from exempting improvements, for surrounding land would yield far more in ground rents. Third, it would strengthen and stabilize greatly the city's finances. All these gains are definite, well established, and proved beyond argument.

Unquestionably some improvement is being worked by public housing, but it is at a terrific expense and often at the expense of private enterprise. Under the program we propose there would be no expense whatever involved to the city and a great impetus would be given to private enterprise, whereas today every public-housing undertaking puts the private operator at a disadvantage.

New residents and new industries would be attracted by the change. Employment would be increased, with immediate activity in the building trades, but this is only the beginning. Heating, plumbing and electric equipment would be called for, and everything which goes into building must be cut, mined, quarried, fabricated and transported. Glass, paint, wallpaper, hardware are needed and, when completed, a house requires carpets, furniture, decoration, refrigerators, radios, clocks and countless gadgets. Finally, new buildings must be serviced by streets, water supply, sewers, transportation, electricity, gas and telephones, and then they must be insured. Building is a basic thing, and whatever helps the construction trades will bring benefit to all industry and to every corner of the land.

The City's Problem

How can this change be simply and painlessly effected? Details of procedure must be worked out for each city, for no two are alike; but a general formula can be worked out, susceptible of modification according to circumstances, and suitable legislation sought.

The principles are simple, but in application there are complications: accurate data are lacking and, pending thorough study, we must work from assessment figures, often far from accurate and not always untainted by fraud. In some cities detailed valuation maps are available, prepared by insurance or realty interests, and these are generally far more accurate than assessment figures. Programs are proposed only in a general way, for the aim is to illustrate broad principles.

An essential consideration in working out a plan for any city is the ratio of improvement values to land values. This determines the increase in levies on land necessary to offset reduction in revenue resulting from exemption of buildings, and guides in deciding how rapidly the change may be put into effect. Generally, this ratio varies widely because of questionable assessment methods. The law often requires separate assessment of land and buildings, but neither assessors nor taxpayers have been educated to understand the significance of these totally different values, and the impression persists that, since the tax is computed only on the total figure, this is all that matters. Often assessors, instead of first determining the value of the site and then the value of the building, estimate the total and then, to comply with what they call "a silly law,'" split this into two items by a haphazard guess.

Generally, higher ratios are found in the smaller cities, for in large centers there is a broader disparity of land values. The differential in desirability of sites is greater, for in one-street villages there is little preference and sites even beyond corporate limits may be worth almost as much as those on Main Street.

Another cause of the wide spread in these ratios lies in the radically different make-up of our cities. Some are compact, close-knit, and congested, while others spraddle all over the countryside. Los Angeles, in pre-war days, had a population density of five to the acre, compared, for instance, with twenty in Philadelphia. It might seem that annexation to the city of broad areas of farm land or wilderness would, by increasing total land values, reduce the ratio of buildings to land, but more often the effect seems to be the opposite, explanation lying in the fact that premature annexation and subdivision depress general land value. Such unsound ventures often mean higher tax rates to cover unwise city improvements, and this, plus increased tax delinquency and forfeiture, can work havoc in land values.

The importance of this ratio should not be exaggerated. Granting that a high ratio is justified and not the result of careless assessment, it is an index to the degree of improvement which may be looked for in *individual* holdings. Unless everything is thrown off balance by speculation, annexation and division, a city showing a high ratio for the city as a whole will tend to show a correspondingly high index of improvement for each developed parcel. Were all properties developed to the same proportionate degree, tax bills would remain unchanged, for untaxing buildings would counterbalance increases on land. It might seem that under such hypothetical and impossible conditions nothing would be accomplished by the change, but actually such a situation would be ideal for reform. No one's tax bill would be either increased or decreased: there would be no opposition to the change and all would be free to build and to improve without incurring any added tax penalty. All would benefit, and the future increment of land values, reflected in ever-increasing ground rents and capitalized by the city, would make possible innumerable desirable and far-reaching public improvements. These would be self-sustaining, self-liquidating and, often, very profitable. Higher ground rents, justified by sound values and real benefits, would be met by property owners without the slightest hardship.

The following pages give a survey of a number of communities, serving to suggest in a general way how we may proceed. Perhaps this preliminary study will lead to thorough research in various localities, including the more progressive cities, to formulate a definite program, blazing a path of action.

Albany as an Example

To illustrate the application of these principles, we offer a detailed study of Albany, not at all as a perfected program, but only as a suggestion. It gives a hint of lines which might be followed in other cities, notably the third-class cities of Pennsylvania. We mention that state because recent legislation makes such a program possible in these cities. State legislation permitting these changes was enacted practically unanimously, inspired by the success of partial reform along these lines in the second-class cities of that state — Pittsburgh and Scranton.

Albany is a city of about 140,000, sixth in size among the cities of New York State and sixty-eighth among American cities, but thirty-first if we use population figures for the metropolitan areas. Like many another city, and especially the older municipalities already "filled up," population gains within municipal limits are moderate, though the metropolitan area shows vigorous growth.

The city is reasonably prosperous but not a boom town nor a war-industry city. It is not much of a manufacturing city, but it is strategically located, with many possibilities as a distributive and administrative center. Its activities are diversified, depending on no one industry. Inclined to conservatism and perhaps a bit slow to accept new ideas, it is above the ordinary in education and intelligence. Like all American cities, it has its blighted areas and slums. Housing needs are average and it contains many old buildings, business and residential, which might well be replaced. It is the writer's home city, of which he has long and intimate knowledge and where he has learned, to his cost, of the difficulties in which real estate owners often find themselves by reason of present tax methods.

In the southeastern section of the city, lying between South Pearl Street and the Hudson River, there is a typical blighted area offering serious hazards of sickness, fire and crime. This district is directly in the path of travel up the Hudson Valley, heading north to Troy, Saratoga, Lake George, the Adirondacks and Canada. Almost the only street available is South Pearl Street, narrow, often obstructed, totally incapable of carrying the traffic and presenting impossible parking conditions.

The proposal is to buy a considerable area, razing the old buildings, constructing a new street and perhaps erecting some modern housing for the workers of the neighborhood. The costs will be met by taxpayers either directly in the city budget or through state and national subsidies, and we have heard no mention of any plan for making it self-liquidating. Apparently the program is being approached in total disregard of fundamental basic principles.

As an alternative South Pearl Street might be widened, taking the east side of the street and making it a thruway, but this would be expensive, difficult and probably not very satisfactory. A better way, and one that would in the long run provide a greatly increased tax revenue to the city, would be to make it possible, by legislation, for the city to levy all local real estate taxes through this broad area, or better yet through all the city, solely on land values, exempting all improvements. Then a fine wide avenue could be opened up, perhaps connecting with an extension going clear through Albany and well on the way to the north, and costs could be met by the greatly increased taxes which would result. With such a vastly improved strip, extending to a considerable distance on both sides of the street, where traffic conditions were excellent and parking facilities abundant, the neighborhood would be vastly improved and values of real estate would be greatly enhanced. Furthermore, this benefit would unquestionably react through a large portion of the city and perhaps through all the city. Exempting new construction from taxation would promote much new building, both industrial and residential.

In the vicinity of this section there were formerly many excellent residences, with the magnificent mansion of General Schuyler of Revolutionary times still standing as an interesting historical shrine. There has also been, in the past, a considerable amount of industry. We recall the country's largest factory of embossed woodenware — checkers, dominoes, childrens' blocks, and the like — and a large and prosperous knitting establishment. There was also a highly profitable specialty factory, a printing and publishing business and a number of other industries, now mostly removed to other cities. The district probably will never recover its position as a favored residential section, but it could be made desirable for workers employed in the neighborhood.

Unquestionably the factors in bringing about the decadence of this neighborhood centered largely on high taxes, the hazards of a slum neighborhood, and traffic difficulties. Considering the trends today, it looks as if the drifting away of industry will still go on unchecked. Two great industrial concerns not very far away, which have long been successful and profitable, have built great plants in another part of the country, and the rumor is that they are to remove permanently. Albany seems to be attracting very few industries.

Why the City Fathers and business interests do not wake up to the benefits of sane tax reform, it is hard to see. It is, or should be, obvious that untaxing improvements will stimulate and attract industry and that a higher levy on land values will discourage holding good sites vacant for speculation. In Pennsylvania there is acute interest, and in parts of New England there is a growing desire to do something to counteract the loss of the textile industries. In several western states, too, there seems to be an awakening, and the Economic Education League, with which the writer is connected, is in constant receipt of requests for information for various parts of the country. Albany has a magnificent opportunity to blaze the way to its own very great advantage.

The least the city should do is to make a thorough study of sound city taxation. Such a study as has been made by Lehigh University of conditions in Bethlehem, Pennsylvania, is called for and it might well cover:

1. The possibility of making such an improvement as proposed, and others like it, self-liquidating, through capitalizing for the city the increased value which it would give to land.

2. The wisdom of following the practice of western cities, in buying vacant and slum properties, converting them for parking, installing meters and leasing them to private operators by competitive bidding.

3. The savings which would result to the city through bettering health, fire, crime and delinquency conditions.

4. Studying the housing problem, which would be solved in a sane businesslike way and without demands on the taxpayers.

5. Attracting new industries.

6. Stabilizing city finances and realty values.

Being the capital of our greatest state, Albany occupies a position more conspicuous than many cities of its size and would serve ideally for a demonstration and example. It has unusual opportunity, and if it will awake to it, the fine old city will enjoy a growth and prosperity such as it has never had in its long history.

Changes in Relative Values

Ten years ago when *The Self-Supporting City* was first published, assessments taken for Albany as a whole showed improvement values and land values to be about equal. Therefore, if we were to exempt improvement values, which practically means building values, we would have had to double the levy on sites to provide the current budget. In preparing this new and revised edition, changes in these figures are necessary. Land is assessed at $101,277,465 and buildings at $188,624,354, a ratio of about 1 to 1.86, almost double the ratio of eight years ago. The increasing ratio of improvement values to site values is something to be considered. It necessitates a greater increase in land-value taxation than would have heretofore been required and, as this increase progresses, it adds to the difficulty of reform but makes it more imperative, for the discouragement to improvement becomes constantly greater and the depression of land values is aggravated.

This change in ratio is significant and appears to prevail the country over. There are three explanations for the increase in the assessed value of buildings as compared with the assessed value of land. One reason is inflation, for builders and building operators face increased cost of everything, as anyone can realize who has to employ even an occasional carpenter, mason, electrician or plumber, and, for reasons into which we cannot enter here, inflation is far more evident in improvement values than in land values. The replacement cost of buildings is much higher than formerly, and assessors assess largely on the basis of replacement costs. Naturally, too, higher cost of building is reflected in the value of all new buildings, and a cursory examination of figures in Albany indicates that the ratio of building values to land values is notably high in the case of new construction, although in many cases older buildings are superior in workmanship, materials and even in design.

The second factor in reducing the relative value of land, as compared with improvements, is the point that we have made again and again, that high taxation of improvements discourages new construction and often makes it impossible to put city land to its best and most profitable use. Indeed it sometimes actually prevents *any* building and therefore it is natural that today values of city land should show a marked relative decline. In the case of some properties, land values have entirely disappeared, as is evidenced by forfeiture for tax delinquency.

In the case of obsolete properties, and districts which real estate men call "blighted areas," including slum properties, land values have declined terrifically, for with the combination of inflation of building costs and the high taxes on buildings — and we believe the latter is far the more potent of these two influences — few can afford to replace the old rookeries with new construction. Remove the tax from the building and this ruinous effect upon land values and land-owners will be ended and there will again be a future for sensible and sane real estate development.

There is a third factor — the simple fact that, although in many cities land values are notably higher, land assessments are often deliberately kept down. The fault is partly that of the assessors. In some states and cities there is a custom of underassessing land, sometimes recognized by city ordinance but often a mere matter of custom, emanating from the idea of going easy on the man who gets no return from his real estate investment. There is all too often a feeling that we shouldn't be too hard on the poor fellow who owns vacant land, or sites occupied by old, dilapidated slum buildings, or any kind of holding which yields practically no cash return. In such cases assessments are frequently ridiculously low. The answer to this problem is to give the owner of such property the opportunity to put it to a profitable use *by not taxing new construction*. Certainly we should not subsidize and perpetuate slums, vacant lots and lots accommodating only billboards, rubbish and dead cats, letting the owner off with a low tax while we penalize those who truly make the city.

We do not say that these forces operate a hundred per cent in Albany. There is building, a good deal of it, but nothing adequate. There is, for example, a dearth of modern, high-class apartments. Changes wrought by time, coupled with the servant question as it affects older people, make it imperative for many now living in big old-fashioned, "downstairs-kitchen" houses to seek more modern and smaller habitations — elevators, up-to-date kitchens, roomy closets and reasonable house service — but the difficulty lies in the expense, *inflated by a tax system which doubles "overhead" costs.* Five per cent interest on building-money loans is all right, but adding another 5 per cent to cover taxes on the building is just one straw too many for the camel's back.

How to Make the Change

This change should not be too difficult: assessments mean little except in connection with tax rates, and if taxpayers understand this they will fuss less over assessments. A change in assessment methods would make a real difference in the relative burden on buildings and on sites, but in itself it would not alter total tax collections.

To effect complete exemption from taxation of all improvements in Albany, maintaining the present tax rate and assuming a constant city budget, we must increase assessment of all taxable land by nearly

$189,000,000, raising present assessments of $101,000,000 to $290,000,-000. Our object is to outline a general method and not to offer an exact schedule, so we use round figures. Precise accuracy is impossible with values and budgets constantly changing, so we multiply site assessments by three for simplicity's sake and incidentally to allow a little margin.

If it should seem unwise to follow so radical a plan, or should difficulty of accomplishing the change look too great, this need offer no discouragement to the program. If necessary, follow more conservative methods. Nearly always, everywhere, today, city land is underassessed, and often grossly so. Frequently the law calls for assessment at 100 per cent, but either local ordinances or custom set assessment figures at 50 per cent or even 25 per cent of full value of land if assessed by our present faulty methods, and in Albany there are many cases of underassessment of land. Our first effort therefore might well be to correct this condition and seek to assess land at the full 100 per cent of selling price if we must follow the ancient customs.

Here again it should be emphasized that this will make it possible to cut the rate on improvement values and that no change in the total tax budget necessarily follows. It would probably be well to embody these two changes in one legislative program, reducing tax rates on improvements in whatever percentage is made possible by the increased levy on sites. Doing this, we believe that, as the tax on improvements is appreciably reduced, the value, and even the sales price, of sites will automatically increase. The policy to be pursued, the details and the figures, depend so much on local conditions that our program should be framed accordingly. Were it properly presented, there should be little opposition, for the majority of taxpayers would profit. It would bring real benefit to the owners of improved property and to those who wish to improve, modernize and develop their holdings, or to replace slums with more profitable buildings. It would be only a small proportion of speculators — those who hold their land idle or ill-used in the hope of an unearned increment — who would suffer.

The state equalization table shows that Albany assessments are on a 63 per cent basis, so land assessments should be raised to $160,000,000 to bring these figures to full valuation even on the present faulty system. To jump land assessments all at once would not be unjust, for it is simply the correction of an inequity, but it would be unwise. Our fallacious method of assessment and of taxation has long been generally accepted, and it seems both wise and fair to effect the change gradually, allowing time for adjustment and avoiding any general upheaval of valuations, prices, taxes and habits of thought. This will make it possible for all to benefit. Holders of vacant land or of inadequately used land can put their holdings on a profitable footing by erecting modern, untaxed housing or by selling to those who will do so, and there will be an opportunity to replace slum buildings with new structures, all untaxed, or to remodel and rebuild without incurring any tax penalty.

We therefore suggest for Albany that the change be made over a period of twenty years. This may seem a long time to wait for a much needed reform, but it is better to go slowly and operate painlessly than to risk confusion and arouse opposition. As each successive step is taken, benefits will become more apparent and it may then prove possible to speed up the process. One point we emphasize: go slowly if you must, *but go all the way*, and plan your program accordingly. Resulting benefits will become increasingly convincing as tax burdens become less oppressive. As taxes are reduced on buildings, improvements will be made, realty in the doldrums restored, and values of sites enhanced, as is demonstrated in Denmark and Australia, where these methods are followed. Gradually one problem after another will be settled: housing will no longer be a costly nightmare; slum areas will be cleared; public improvements will be made on a basis profitable to the city; finances will be stabilized and we shall create a better city.

Modifications of this program in some of the details has often been proposed. The writer formerly advocated an increase of the tax rate on land values, but the experience of some Canadian cities, as well as theoretical study, leads to the conviction that provision for increase of assessments is the better answer. One vital argument lies in the point already made — that otherwise, as we increase the tax rate on sites, their *assessed value* may be completelly obliterated. By raising assessments as suggested, we shall bring these figures to the full value of land and we shall establish a basis for ground-rent collection which is both stable and honest.

As for our terminology, there has been much bickering about whether to phrase this proposal as collecting ground rent or a tax on land values. The former designation is more accurate and yet, for legal reasons, it may be advisable to use the more common phrasing and speak of a tax on land (or site) values. For this there are two reasons: there is a natural resentment at any proposal to make a landowner pay ground rent on a site which he, in ignorance of custom and law, imagines he owns outright in the same sense in which he owns his watch. There may also be technical legal difficulties in collecting ground rent for the support of government. Taxation is understood, recognized and accepted, but rent collection may be another story, and it has been suggested that a proposal so phrased might sometimes involve the necessity of constitutional change. However, this is a secondary consideration, for legislation, or perhaps constitutional change, will be called for in any event.

Should it become necessary to provide for greater budgets, the answer is to continue this process of increasing land assessments, never under any circumstances reverting to the taxation of improvements. Even if demands become excessive, they will be far more readily carried by sites than by buildings. Today we see in cities the country over good and potentially serviceable buildings being torn down because it is cheaper to destroy them than to pay taxes on them. Often it would be possible to find tenants for them at a fair rental — but not high enough to cover the crushing taxation and still leave a fair return to the owner. But the site? That can't be destroyed however high we tax it, and a high tax on the land serves to force it into profitable, untaxed use.

A marked increase in legal land assessments can be justified on several scores: (1) these assessments are frequently made, perfectly openly, at only a mere fraction of the correct valuations, (2) since land values are directly and closely tied with improvement exemption, as the latter progresses, land values automatically rise, and (3) taxation of values created by the common life, even if excessive — but we deny that they would be — are less objectionable and go less against our moral sense than does the outright seizure of values created by personal initiative, in buildings and comparable improvements, framed on the philosophy of the gangster, taking, with absolutely no moral justification, values which are the product of individual private life and labor.

Experience in Pennsylvania shows that there need be little difficulty in securing enabling legislation if the wisdom of discrimination between these two classes of values and its justice are demonstrated. Taxation of improvements must always discourage building and add to the cost of housing both people and industry; but, no matter how oppressive are the exactions of ground rent, we shall not reduce the size of the globe by a single inch. However, we repeat once more that we have no reason to believe that such levies shall need to become excessive.

We favor such increase of assessments, rather than of tax rates, except perhaps in exceptional cases where tax rates are notably low, as in the city of Washington, where it would doubtless become possible to raise the rate if this seems preferable. Little as we like the income tax and much as a general sales tax is to be decried, either of these evils is to be preferred to any step which will prolong our terrible housing problem and hamper commercial life. These lesser evils are to be preferred to condemning millions of our people to habitations scarcely fit for swine. This is, however, an academic question for, without getting into state or federal questions, there is not the slightest doubt that, were our cities to collect full ground rent, exempting all improvements, their finances would be far stronger and local sales and income taxes could be abolished. Should such a system fail to meet the city budget, the answer is to cut the budget.

A Long-time Program

The following table shows how the proposed program would operate in Albany, if spaced over twenty years. Note that the total tax yield, $13,000,000, remains approximately constant, in round figures, but tax rates on improvements are steadily reduced until wholly eliminated. The rate on land is kept constant at the present figure, but the assessments are increased by 10 per cent of present assessments each year. Up to the sixth year these increases are justified by the present state equalization table, for they are necessary to bring these figures up to the full 100 per cent valuation required by law, even under our present faulty system. Then, since half of the true value is lodged in the

Albany
Tax Yield from All Land & Buildings in Millions

Year	Land Assessed Value	Yield	Buildings Tax Rate	Yield	Total Tax Yield
Now	100	4.50	4.5	8.3700	12.870
1st	110	4.95	4.275	7.9515	12.902
2nd	120	5.40	4.050	7.5330	12.933
3rd	130	5.85	3.825	7.1145	12.965
4th	140	6.30	3.600	6.6960	12.996
5th	150	6.75	3.375	6.2775	13.025
6th	160	7.20	3.150	5.8590	13.059
7th	170	7.65	2.925	5.4405	13.091
8th	180	8.10	2.700	5.0220	13.122
9th	190	8.55	2.475	4.6035	13.155
10th	200	9.00	2.250	4.1850	13.185
11th	210	9.45	2.025	3.7665	13.216
12th	220	9.90	1.800	3.3480	13.248
13th	230	10.35	1.575	2.9295	13.280
14th	240	10.80	1.350	2.5110	13.311
15th	250	11.25	1.125	2.0925	13.343
16th	260	11.70	.900	1.6740	13.374
17th	270	12.15	.675	1.2555	13.406
18th	280	12.60	.450	.8370	13.437
19th	290	13.05	.225	.4185	13.469
20th	300	13.50	0	0	13.500

city, we are justified in doubling this figure, thus bringing it to 320. An increase to 300 will be sufficient to yield revenue to counterbalance the full exemption of improvements.

Doubtless, by the end of twenty years, the demands of the city will have increased materially and, in such a case, the further increase of these land assessments will be justified, for, with complete exemption of improvements and general betterment of the city, land values will have increased considerably beyond these figures. If not, the tax rate can be raised or, far better, the city budget cut, and this should be easily possible. Housing subsidies will be eliminated, tax delinquency greatly reduced and many expenses of the municipal government, notably the defensive services of sanitation, fire and police, will be cut because of decent housing. Remember, too, that the cost of many civic improvements, now generally a dead charge on taxpayers, will be self-liquidating and often profitable because of their reaction on ground rents.

The immediate question in the mind of almost everyone, when a tax change is proposed, is what will it do to his tax bill. The next table shows how this plan would affect various classes of property according to the degree in which they are improved, as shown by the relation between improvement and site values. These changes would be made annually, but for simplicity and to save space we summarize the results, showing them only for each five years. How the tax on vacant land, devoid of improvements, will operate is shown by the first three columns of the table already given. It is apparent that this tax, or more accurately the collection of ground rent by the city, will increase each year, being trebled at the end of the twenty-year period. If this seems drastic, remember that the owners of such properties do nothing whatever, *as landowners*, for the city. They employ no one, house no one and add nothing to the city, sitting idly by while their unused land increases in value because of the services and contributions of all the people. Remember, too, that they can, if they will, be compensated for this added levy on their holdings by the opportunity to put them to profitable untaxed use and that, doing this, they will be far better off.

There will be far less speculative inflation of land prices, for land will be bought for use and not in the hopes of speculative gain. Land will be forced on the market and it will be easier for would-be builders and homeowners to acquire sites: yet experience in other lands has shown that generally the first effect of the acceptance of such a program is to increase land prices, because, with a prospect of building untaxed homes, there is a far more lively demand for sites. Here again is an argument for spreading the change over some years: it gives an opportunity to landowners to protect themselves.

What Classes Benefit the Most

In this table we give figures for Albany based on holdings (1. where the value of improvements is equal to the value of the site, (2) where the value of improvements to site value is as 1.89 to 1 (this being the approximate average for the city as a whole), representing the class of property which will be least affected. Then we follow with tables of properties of a ratio of 3 to 1, 5 to 1, 10 to 1 and 20 to 1.

There are some points to which attention should be called. Note that in every case the levy on site (or the ground rent collected by the city) increases steadily at a fixed rate and uniformly for all classes of property, and that finally all the tax on improvements is eliminated. Obviously bare land shows the greatest increase in its tax bill, and tax savings increase as the proportion of improvement values, as compared with sites, increases. This is to be expected, for the tax on buildings today increases with their value, and so the amount saved by elimination of this tax is greatest where the present-day tax is greatest.

The second table, representing property which is approximately average and may be said to be typical, shows practically no change in tax bills, some trivial variation being due to the dropping of decimals and use of approximate figures. It may be said that the program will not affect these owners, but that is a superficial interpretation. Their properties show inadequate development and, being only average, doubtless many are more or less obsolete and run down and not up to today's needs and demands. Presumably, although they may be earning some return, they are not very profitable and clamor for improvement, modernization or perhaps replacement by new buildings meeting today's standards. That these improvements are not made now is due to the heavy tax penalty imposed on those who improve their properties. Under the proposed plan, when such operations bring no increase in tax costs, they can and will be profitably made in many cases.

As a practical matter it is generally found that the classes of properties showing the least *immediate* benefit are holdings encumbered with residences or commercial buildings which have outlived their usefulness and which should be replaced. There are often serious hazards from health and fire standpoints and frequently cost the city dearly in protective services or in loss of life. For them, the program offers vast future possibilities.

Good modern housing often shows the highest ratio of improvement values, and more particularly the smaller and more modest homes, because residences of the ten-to-thirty-thousand-dollar class often stand on comparatively low-priced sites and show a broader ratio of improve-

Albany

Tax Changes, per $100 of present site assessments, by ratio of improvements to sites, given by 5-year intervals

Year	Ratio 1 to 1			Ratio 1.86 to 1		
	Site Tax	Bldg. Tax	Total	Site Tax	Bldg. Tax	Total
Now	4.50	4.50	9.00	4.50	8.370	12.87
5th	6.75	3.38	10.13	6.75	6.278	13.03
10th	9.00	2.25	11.25	9.00	4.185	13.185
15th	11.25	1.125	12.38	11.25	2.09	13.34
20th	13.50	0	13.50	13.50	0	13.50

Year	Ratio 3 to 1			Ratio 5 to 1		
Now	4.50	13.50	18.00	4.50	22.50	27.00
5th	6.75	10.13	16.88	6.75	16.88	23.63
10th	9.00	6.75	15.75	9.00	11.25	20.25
15th	11.25	3.38	14.63	11.25	5.63	16.88
20th	13.50	0	13.50	13.50	0	13.50

Year	Ratio 10 to 1			Ratio 20 to 1		
Now	4.50	45.00	49.50	4.50	90.00	94.50
5th	6.75	33.75	40.50	6.75	67.50	74.25
10th	9.00	22.50	31.50	9.00	45.00	54.00
15th	11.25	11.25	22.50	11.25	22.50	33.75
20th	13.50	0	13.50	13.50	0	13.50

ment values than do the more pretentious residences. Frequently, too, the newer, better and larger industrial buildings and factories show a high ratio; but, if it be said that therefore our program favors "big business," we remind the reader that new, progressive and profitable industries, located in modern, safe and comfortable buildings, are earnestly desired by most cities. It is on such enterprises that the workingman is largely dependent for his job, prosperity and better way of living. More and more there is a tendency for industry to move out of old firetraps in the congested part of the cities and relocate in new and modern buildings in less congested sections. Frequently industries move beyond city limits, and even to distant towns and cities, to escape high taxes, resulting often in serious loss of tax revenue. Eliminate land speculation and building taxation and this exodus from cities will tend to stop.

While this example is based on the city of Albany, the same general plan could be applied to practically any American city. In many, where they suffer from abominations which Albany has thus far escaped, such as personal property taxes, sales taxes and city income taxes, it will be desirable to continue the process further, to eliminate such taxes which are far more objectionable by every count than would be increasing ground rent.

It is desirable to keep building assessments at present levels, and the best way to get rid of taxes is to reduce the tax rate on improvements steadily for twenty years. The mathematics is simple. The present tax rate is 4.50 and we propose to eliminate it, as applied to buildings, entirely in twenty years. Therefore, we reduce this rate by one twentieth or by 0.225 each year and, by doing this, the decrease in tax receipts from this source will be directly counterbalanced by increased receipts resulting from the steadily increasing assessments of site values. Thus our tax revenue remains almost constant, as will be seen by adding the figures for each year in the second and fourth columns of our first table, on page 49.

Some Specific Albany Illustrations

In the first edition of this book we worked out in considerable detail just how the proposed change would affect tax bills on a good many pieces of Albany property. Since that time there have been many changes in assessments, valuations and tax rates, but it hardly seems worth while to go over this again in detail, especially as statistical data are always changing.

In broad general terms there would be a very considerable saving on the tax bill in the case of the big modern office buildings, of which Albany has altogether too few. The hotels would also pay a good deal less, and the great telephone building would show a tremendous reduction in tax costs. These are all modern buildings of which the value greatly exceeds the value of the site.

Albany is full of old office buildings, inconvenient, obsolete, generally walk-ups and frequently bad fire risks. The writer himself occupied an office in one such building not very long ago, located in a splendid location in the heart of the city, but the building had long outlived its usefulness. This property underwent many changes of ownership, with mortgages, foreclosures, compromises and what not, and finally one owner undertook to "improve" it with flimsy and dangerous ornamental woodwork trim, shoddy and presenting a serious fire hazard. We protested this fire hazard to city authorities and to the underwriters but without effect and, accordingly, we moved our office. Shortly after, the building burned with the loss of two lives. This is just an illustration of the tragedy which often results from the perpetuation of old and dangerous buildings preserved by the blind tax policies of our cities.

[53]

It may be worth while to review some of the figures given for residential properties in our first edition — one based on the writer's own experience. He inherited the old family residence, which had been a fine old house, on one of Albany's best streets, but the march of progress had ended one-family occupancy of such residences and the district was being given over to semi-business, professional offices, "shoppes," boarding and rooming houses, with the old homes converted by makeshift alterations. When the writer owned it, the site was assessed at $15,000 and the house, made over for roomers, at $7,000, allowance being made for obsolescence. The tax bill was about $900, and for years the property struggled to meet it with indifferent success. Three times it had changed hands by virtual foreclosure, selling the last time for a mere fraction of its assessed value, although the same property had sold for $40,000 just before the collapse of 1929.

When we studied it in detail a few years ago the tax bill on this property would have been increased by about $35 each year under our proposed plan, and at the end of ten years it would have been about $350 higher than today, but the owner would have been far better off. Again and again thought was given to replacing the old home by a modern apartment house, but always it was the same story: taxes would eat up most of the earnings. Under a sensible tax plan, it would have been quite otherwise. What would an increase of $350 in the tax bills signify if an untaxed apartment house could earn a liberal return? The site is deep and wide, running through to another good residential street, the rear lot vacant and earning nothing; the combined holding could easily have justified at least a $500,000 development if untaxed. It would have been ideal for an apartment house and, with the cost of building as it is today, we believe that this property would have become a profitable investment and a sure instead of a most uncertain source of tax revenue to the city. Such a building would unquestionably have been erected on this lot had it not been for our tax folly, and it would have meant a substantial contribution to much-needed housing, as well as an increased tax yield to the city.

When this book was written we also made a study of a number of other houses with which the writer happened to be familiar. We do not think the situation has changed materially. In one case a house valued at $17,500 and taxed at $700 would have paid just about half its present taxes and for a third property, typical of many, where the house is worth $10,000 on a lot worth something over $2,000, the tax bill would have been cut from $500 to $167. In another case, the home of a workingman, the tax bill would have been reduced by enough to save the owner sufficient to cover both interest and the amortization of a mortgage for more than half the cost of the home.

And the Speculator?

In this city there are many holdings in less highly developed sections where lots are vacant and tax-delinquent. With buildings untaxed, there would be a sale for such lots: many a home would go up and tax collections would be assured, and much-needed homes for low-income families would displace dumps, billboards and ragweed. Another example studied was a preamature subdivision of building lots assessed at about $400 each. A very few are occupied by houses assessed at about $6,000 and taxed at about $280 a year, the taxes about equal to interest on their cost. Most of the lots are still vacant and taxed at $20, and nearly all are delinquent and in forfeiture. They are worth nothing either to owner or city, as long as houses are prohibitively taxed, for they yield no income and pay no taxes. Untax improvements and houses would spring up like mushrooms and these lots, yielding nothing today in taxes, would be again productive of tax revenue. Such instances could be multiplied indefinitely and they show clearly how the effect of the taxation of buildings is to destroy the value of land and to continue to aggravate the housing problem.

The way to clean up the whole difficulty is to untax all buildings. Tax the vacant lot the same as the next lot which carries a building, and the vacant lot will not long stand idle. Who would continue to maintain an old rattery, vacant or half vacant, or occupied by fly-by-night tenants paying—or more often jumping—the rent, were it possible to erect a modern building for responsible, respectable tenants without increasing tax costs? Slums would be replaced by modern housing, and good and useful buildings would no longer be torn down, as they are today, to save tax bills, letting the lots stand idle and vacant.

If there is neither building nor sale, our program might add to the plight of some owners, for seldom can an unwise purchaser, buying at inflated, speculative prices, save himself. Injury may result to some playing a losing game, but should our policy be framed for their protection? If an obstinate holder refuses to sell or utilize his holding, there are two possibilities. He may continue to hold, retarding the development of the city, ultimately profiting by what others do, or he may hold indefinitely, sending good money after bad, until he finally loses all. In any event the city loses: either the property is dropped from the tax books or the owner reaps a harvest which justly belongs to the city. The owner of the modest home, or the man who wants to become a homeowner, will gain, and gain far more proportionately than do the owners of great buildings, and remember that whatever helps the borrower helps the lender. Freeing buildings will reduce "rents" and do much for tenants.

In such a city as Albany there should be little difficulty in effecting such a change were an effort made to educate the public to its benefits. There would be opposition — we always growl about taxes — but every objection could be answered and change would come gradually with ample time for adjustment by building or selling. Probably the greatest problem would be that of the old business structures to which we have referred, uncomfortable and involving grave fire hazards. We can hardly hope that they will all be razed overnight to make way for modern buildings, although, allowing time, that might happen in many cases, for old rookeries often occupy excellent sites. Probably the answer would generally be rebuilding and modernization. However these problems are met, it is only common sense to give every inducement to improvement rather than to follow a policy which results in razing good serviceable buildings to give way to wretched little "taxpayers" of only a story or two.

The Assessment of Improvements

Even if taxation no longer necessitates assessment to buildings, they should nevertheless be assessed at full value for other reasons, just as today we customarily assess the values of tax-exempt buildings. Sometimes other taxes, such as school, county, and state levies, are based on assessments and include buildings; and, while every effort shoud be made sooner or later to eliminate such taxes, by the same process by which we propose to end city taxes, it may be years before such a reform can be effected. Assessed values are also frequently a determining factor in limiting public borrowing and sometimes form a basis for the distribution of state funds. It will be policy to leave present improvement assessments pretty much unchanged and under no circumstances to increase them. Reduction will be desirable whenever any reason develops because of deterioration or obsolescence, and of course in the case of fire or destruction. Rebuilding, improving and modernizing existing structures should bring no increase of assessment.

And New Buildings

There are several ways of meeting the question of the erection of new buildings, particularly industrial plants. In about three quarters of our states concessions are offered to new industries locating within their borders, sometimes openly and legally but frequently illegally but by general consent, because of their value to the community. These plans work: they do attract industry and are a potent factor in drawing factories to new locations, particularly in the South, but in the writer's opinion they are unwise. It is dangerous and demoralizing to encourage and abet assessment practices which are illegal. The best way to meet such a situation is to enforce the law uncompromisingly, and often the result is a reaction which makes repeal easy. Another objection, and a serious one, is that it puts owners of property already improved at a marked disadvantage. It is similar to the question of public housing, which subjects private enterprise to unfair competition. Those who have anticipated the needs of our city, whether residential or commercial, are forced to pay higher taxes because of the tax exemption granted to rivals. There should be justice with no discrimination.

A Tax Option for Builders

We believe the best way to meet this question is to permit any owner of real estate so desiring, and entirely at his option, to put his property at once on the tax basis established at the completion of the proposed plan, provided that such a course does not reduce his present tax bill. Let the newcomer, whether a resident or a business, buy his site, put his holding under the new law based on the last line of our tabular schedule, and then erect his home, his factory or whatever it may be, without incurring any increase in taxation. Should land values increase beyond that assessed, he would of course be subject to payment of higher ground rent, but with no reference whatever to improvements made by the owner. Often building and development will increase all land values in the neighborhood, and these conditions should be taken into consideration in fixing ground rents — just another illustration of how the owner of land benefits by what others do — but this is a totally different matter from improvements made on his particular piece of property.

The exercise of such an option would not reduce the tax income of the city, for, though the new factory is not taxed, the ground rent of the site would be multiplied by three. True, the tax would be less than it would be under today's plan if the new building is erected, but probably it will not be erected on present tax terms. However it may be in isolated instances, experience clearly demonstrates that with tax exemption many new factories will be attracted which, under the usual conditions of today, will not be built or which will be located elsewhere. There are indications that one explanation of the flight of industry to the South is that there they are granted tax exemption denied to them in the North.

A provision of this sort, encouraging the immediate improvement of property and indirectly of the city, would give an impetus to the program. In some rapidly growing cities the example and the obvious benefits would be so apparent that many owners of land already somewhat improved would seek to take advantage of it. This might easily make it possible to speed up the program.

The Case of New York City

The principles and methods suggested for Albany might be applied in another and greater city. Taking New York City for example, we see much the same situation: the ratio of building to land values was about 1.1 ten years ago and now it is about 1.64 to 1 and, if we add to the building values the franchise values, the ratio is 1.79 to 1.

The reason for including franchise values is that practically the tax on franchises is, in many ways, similar to the tax on improvements. The franchise represents a privilege, frequently an exclusive privilege, of using the streets in conducting public service business. To tax it has much the same effect as taxing improvement values, for it necessarily raises the cost of such indispensable public services as transportation, communication, light, heat, etc., to the public, and these items are a far more serious factor in the budget of the poor man than in that of the wealthy.

In theory, the rates and services of the public utilities are subject to regulation, supposedly fixed in a way which will be fair to the company and at the same time prevent exploitation of the public. Therefore, if the cost of operations is increased by a franchise tax, this cost is necessarily passed on to the ultimate consumer; and, if the franchise tax is abolished, it should result in lower prices for these necessary things. The problem, therefore, resolves itself into the question of whether we wish to raise revenue by a tax which increases the cost of the necessities of life or whether the price of these things should be kept just as low as possible. We believe that in a great city like New York it would pay to treat the franchise values just as we treat the improvement values.

It may be asked why the taxation of franchises is not a factor in every city and why we mention it only in connection with New York City. As a matter of fact, the argument as we apply it to the great metropolis would apply anywhere, but in many small cities it is of minor importance and tax and assessment figures as they affect franchises are not always readily available. In most cities it might be as well to concentrate on the greater reform of untaxing buildings and postpone the franchise tax question for the present.

The Situation in New York

New York city presents much the same problem as do our smaller cities but, being bigger, its problems are greater and more involved. As in most cities, taxes and finances are a worry and the city is often in serious financial jams. Traffic and transit are problems made more acute by the fact that the city is built upon a long and relatively narrow island. Except for that of the national government, its budget is the greatest in the nation, but in financial supremacy the city is slipping, its percentage of the banking funds and assets of the nation shows a steady decline and its export trade has slumped sharply. Real estate and other levies show an increase.

The program outlined would do much to aid the city. Housing needs and slum clearance would be solved by a simple tax change, encouraging building and checking the inflation of land prices, for there would be little temptation to hold land idle or inadequately used, in the hope of speculator's profit. To reduce traffic congestion Senator Desmond has wisely proposed the tax exemption of garages, which would aid in keeping cars off the streets, but it is odd that the distinguished senator confines his argument to the housing of cars: exactly the same program, applied to buildings, would aid in housing us, and it would seem that housing our people is as much to be sought as housing our cars.

This tax program would meet these needs of our cities without expense and would be a step toward stabilizing finances and relieving the oppressed taxpayer. It would certainly be a far wiser program than the recent proposal to raise a housing fund by taxing every telephone in the city two dollars a year or to increase the sales tax, which has already driven considerable business out of the city.

An increased levy on site values would make it far easier for the city to acquire land at reasonable figures and would react to facilitate ending the twin evils of slum clearance and parking difficulties.

A Tentative Suggestion

The following table shows in the first column the ratio of improvement values to land values, by boroughs and for the city as a whole. In the second column it gives a similar ratio but includes, with the improvement values, franchise values. These ratios are on the basis of these values as compared with each $100 valuation of land.

We give these simple ratios rather than detailed figures, which would be confusing, running into billions, and we do not work them out to exact decimal points. Our idea is to outline a method rather than to give a detailed schedule, seeking to show an approximation to conditions and principles rather than an exact statistical study of conditions which are in constant flux.

In the entire city as a whole the ratio of improvement values to land values is 164 to 100. Including franchise values with improvement values, this ratio is raised to 179.3. We propose, tentatively, spreading the change over ten years, eliminating all taxation of improvement values in that period and increasing the levy on land values, so that the total tax revenue of the city will remain unchanged. To accomplish this, we propose reducing the tax rate on buildings by one tenth of the present figure, in successive years and then elminating the tax on improvements entirely.

To compensate for this loss of revenue the tax on land values must be increased by 164 per cent of what they are now. Spreading the change over ten years, we would increase these taxes by 16.4 per cent each year by increasing land assessments by this ratio, keeping the rate unchanged. It is better, and we believe wholly justified, to increase assessments on land, but in reducing taxes on buildings we would cut the rate, keeping assessments as they are. Following such a method, at the end of ten years taxes on improvements would be entirely eliminated and levies on sites would be increased sufficiently to counterbalance this reduction, so the budget would be unchanged.

Should it be desired to include the elimination of the franchise taxes, use the figures in the second column in this table.

If it is desired to spread the change over twice as long, covering twenty years, cut the rate of reduction of the tax rate on improvements and increase land valuations by half.

If possible to effect the change by boroughs, details can be worked out from this table following this general procedure.

To forestall criticism we repeat once more that we are convinced that such increases in the valuation of land would be thoroughly justifiable, for as the use of land is untaxed the value of land increases. Furthermore, very often land is today underassessed on any basis.

RATIO OF IMPROVEMENT AND FRANCHISE VALUES TO EACH $100 OF SITE VALUE

	Improvements	Improvements plus Franchises
Entire City	164	179.3
Manhattan	121	157.5
Bronx	210	226.5
Brooklyn	202	216.4
Queens	246	258.6
Richmond	183	195.4

We give computations for each of the boroughs of Greater New York as well as figures for the entire city. Whether the change should be attempted for the city as a whole or for selected boroughs, we do not know. That is a question of practical politics. If possible to do it by boroughs and if one single borough were to act, it would doubtless force the others to follow suit. Were the entire city to adopt this program, the influence of its example would be felt the world over. As a practical measure we believe it would be wisest to plan for a campaign of twenty years, for it would be well to allow plenty of time for adjustment and for popular education rather than to risk jeopardizing the program by rushing it too much.

No matter how we go about it or how cautiously we move, there is sure to be some opposition, because there always is to any proposal for tax changes. We might arouse something of a howl about letting the "great corporations" off too easily and putting all the burden on "the common man" were we to include the franchises in our reform, but this we think is nonsense, for with the easing of the tax burdens of the public utility companies correlated with reduced rates and better service, with lower charges for transportation, gas, electricity and telephones, the benefit to all would be apparent. The burden would be far more easily carried and the change would not oppress industry, choke progress and close the door on the expansion of jobs.

It looks as if the substitution of socialism for private enterprise is bearing the usual bitter fruit in an excessive cost of electric power developed by city plants. Some years ago the Edison Company offered to buy these plants from the city, modernize them and sell electricity to the city, but nothing came of these negotiations, so $100,000,000 was spent in an inefficient rebuilding of the obsolete plants. The upshot is that the cost of electricity produced in these plants is about twice what the electricity would cost if purchased from the Edison Company, meaning an annual waste, it is said, of about $7,500,000. The transit authorities are asking for $17,000,000 more for improvements, and it looks as if another $100,000,000 might go down the drain before anything approaching a satisfactory job is achieved. Even then the costs of operation will unquestionably exceed the costs of purchasing electricity.

This discussion may seem alien to our general argument, but it all bears upon questions of city finance and economies which might be effected. The transit situation in New York is too complicated to be summed up briefly, but it is the writer's impression that, were the city to collect through the collection of ground rent a return on the great advance of land values which has followed the building of the subways, and if there were a serious effort to get away from socialistic city ownership, there would be a good chance of putting the subway situation upon a reasonably safe financial foundation.

Some critics will say that our proposed program would result in over building. More will be said on these angles of the case, but it is obvious that there could be a great deal of building before we overdo decent, modern, up-to-date, sanitary housing for our people. As for overbuilding and the threat which some see of filling up the area of a great city with skyscrapers, with no spaces, parks or sunshine, it could be forestalled in large part if the city were to buy up slums and unimproved properties, which would unquestionably be forced on the market by increased tax bills, and convert such holdings into parking lots or breathing spots. They could be developed for parking in the manner followed by a California city, razing slums and obsolete buildings, filling in, grading and servicing the area, equipping it with parking meters and opening it to general public parking; or let the land by competitive bidding to a concessionaire to operate for public parking. If it seems hard that some land will be forced on the market by this proposal, remember that it is entirely up to the owners: they can take advantage of the law and profit by it if they wish, putting their land to productive, profitable and sensible use.

Unquestionably a far greater development of the city would be possible and profitable when untaxed than we envision today. Flight to the suburbs would be checked and constant improvements, better housing, less congestion, cheaper and more satisfactory transit to and from jobs and a relief in traffic and parking would be reflected in higher land values, making the increased levies on the land not at all burdensome.

The Pennsylania Cities

Pennsylvania is losing a great opportunity. The city of Philadelphia, the only first-class city in the state, is a law unto itself. The second-class cities, Pittsburgh and Scranton, long ago accepted a partial plan on the lines indicated. In Pittsburgh it has been a success. In Scranton not much has been accomplished, but there are conditions having nothing whatever to do with taxes — notably the slump in the anthracite coal market — that make Scranton an unfortunate guinea pig by which to test the plan. All the other cities are third-class cities, and a study of census figures shows very little growth and in the past ten years nearly half the cities show a loss of population. The state government is making an effort to attract new industries. Apparently they feel that they are badly needed, but they do not see the simple expedient which the new law makes possible and which would do much to bring industry to their state. It may be worth while to consider some of the difficulties which have been brought up in Pennsylvania.

It is sometimes said that putting the burden on land would have been fine if the change had been made before land acquired value — in other words, when it would have yielded nothng — but now it is unfair because owners have bought their land in good faith. This is nonsense. If our proposal would have been valid when Adam and Eve left the Garden of Eden it is valid today. Because we have long blundered is no reason why we should continue to blunder and go on letting the speculator pocket the return on an ever-increasing value of land, brought about and paid for by all society.

Consider the enormous increase in land values in New York, Chicago, Los Angeles, Detroit or even entire states such as California or Florida, all the result of (1) growth of population, (2) public services rendered by the government and paid for by the taxpayers and (3) general social advance, invention and progress. Should we let the unearned profits from these increased values go into private pockets for all time and force our cities into confiscating a large part of the earnings of buildings which are justly private property? Frequently the tax collector collects practically all of the earnings of the buildings, and that is why we see good and serviceable housing torn down the whole country over to cut tax bills. Which is the wiser and more ethical: to take for common use the earnings of society and of government, as measured by ground rent, or to seize the earnings of personal life and labor?

The argument that it would be unjust to shift the tax because it would reduce the value of investments in land made in good faith is indefensible, for such an argument would defeat any change in the incidence of taxation. Must society always remain static because change will hurt some group? As a matter of fact, the change advocated would bring great benefit to many a land speculator: to profit by it, it is only necessary to put his land to use instead of holding it idle, blocking progress and seeking to reap where others sow. Remember, too, that it is only by taxing the land itself that we can untax what is done in, on and to the land, so it resolves itself into a question of whether we penalize those who truly make our cities, supplying housing, cleaning up slums and giving employment, or give the advantage to the dog-in-the-manger who will neither use his land nor sell it to one who will.

There are, we admit, practical difficulties, but these should not prove insurmountable. In Pennsylvania, which is something of a key state because of its permissive law, we see three major problems. There is a law prohibiting a tax rate in excess of fifteen mills, but this could be met by changing the law and raising this limitation or even doing away with it as far as it applies to land values, and we could balance any increase on land by lowering the tax-rate limit on improvement values or abolishing all such taxation after a few years. A better way might be to secure legislation making possible the assessment of land at its true value, as has been pointed out, basing it upon the rent it commands and not upon the selling price of the fractional equity lodged with the titleholder.

A second obstacle to be overcome is the unfortunate fact that, in Pennsylvania, school taxes and county taxes on city property are things quite apart from the regular municipal tax. Sometimes the school levy is as great as the regular city tax, and frequently school and county taxes combined exceed the municipal tax. These taxes, school and county are not affected by city legislation and therefore, under present laws, it is impossible to put the proposed reform into full effect, for it could only be about a 50 per cent measure. Sometimes, as in the case of Bethlehem, there are practical political problems, for that city lies in two counties of different classification and includes several school districts of various classes.

The answer to this is to require that school and county taxes be levied on the basis of assessments made for regular municipal taxation, or it might be wise to seek a general state law requiring that school and county taxes be graded in the same way as the regular city tax. A better way might be to require that the city's share of the county and school taxes should be levied *against the city*, permitting the city to levy taxes for schools and county in the same manner as the municipal tax.

Another way to meet this question of practical difficulties would be to make the change by the optional method already suggested. This would make the transition slowly, but we believe that the immediate benefit of those taking advantage of it would prove a very convincing lesson to others and thus facilitate the full realization of the program.

The method would be to compute, as of today, the percentage of increase in ground rents necessary to free absolutely all improvement values from taxation, putting the entire burden on site values, working out these figures for the city as a whole. Then, if the property owner so elects, permit him to place his property immediately on this new tax basis, paying the required rate on site values and nothing whatever on improvement values, with the single proviso that this option should be conditional upon its effecting no reduction in his present tax bill. Taking advantage of this opportunity would mean that he could displace an old firetrap with modern housing or that he could build on a vacant lot or that he could improve his property and put it in shape and make it truly profitable without incurring any further tax. Avoiding the increase which he would normally have to pay under today's plan would usually offset the increase in the levy on the site.

This might perhaps be the best way and the safest way to put the plan into effect and to work a tremendous improvement. Although for a time it might go slowly, we believe that the example and demonstration would soon make it popular and make the effect pretty general throughout the city.

In all honesty, and after some forty years of thought and study, the writer is convinced that the plan would work to the benefit of practically every class of our people with the single exception of the obstinate speculator who persists in holding land vacant or inadequately used in the hope of profiting by what others do.

One aspect of the question is frequently overlooked. In our blindness today we are spending many millions of dollars on so-called public housing. The bills for this unnecessary extravagance are met largely by the owners of properties destined to suffer by the unfair competition which the untaxed public housing offers to private enterprise. By a sane policy of taxation all this so-called public housing, being housing for which one man pays and from which another man benefits, would be rendered entirely unnecessarily. Our housing and slum problems would be readily met by free private enterprise operating with profit.

That high taxes in Pennsylvania are often a factor in checking industrial development is apparent. We know of one case where a really large concern, known the world over, is considering moving to a neighboring state because, under Pennsylvania law, their taxes are much more oppressive than those of their leading competitor located where laws are far more favorable. The removal of this business would be a blow to Pennsylvania and would damage its prestige. After talking with the president of the company the writer is convinced that these difficulties would be ended if the simple changes which we advocate were made. Not only would it greatly reduce the taxes on the industrial plants of the company but it would also reduce taxes on the homes of their employees, and a very large proportion of their workers own their own homes. This business is in a serious quandary, and the state would do well to act before it is too late.

In another part of the country we find a similar situation. In New England industries have closed up and moved away, and this is notably true in the textile field, where many have gone South, influenced in part by the lower wage scale but very largely by more favorable tax laws. Many of the little cities of New England are in a precarious position and are well aware of it. We believe that were they to follow a more enlightened plan of taxation, especially as applied to industrial properties, many of their troubles would be over. They are working through departments of commerce and chambers of commerce and voluntary organizations, trying to attract new industries, and often offer concessions far more expensive than the simple change which we propose. Is it not worth while for cities such as these to consider

[65]

a plan which has accomplished wonders in countries where it has been tried, notably in Denmark and Australia and to a lesser extent in New Zealand?

A Program for New Jersey

The State of New Jersey issues an excellent and comprehensive report, through its Division of Taxation, which gives a much clearer picture than is often obtainable. It shows for the state at large a value of the assessed land of about $1,600,000,000 and of improvements thereon of about five billion. Beside this tax on realty the state also has a most objectionable tax on "tangible personal property" divided into four categories, household goods, farm equipment, stock in trade and in manufacture and "all other personal property," assessed at about a billion dollars. Such taxation has been described as a cross between guesswork and perjury, for it is impossible to assess it with any degree of accuracy, and opportunities for corruption and collusion are unlimited.

Apparently in New Jersey assessments are vague and hit-or-miss. It is reported that in Monmouth County they range from 3 per cent to 80 per cent of true value. In Hoboken they are on a 70 per cent basis, but in some south Jersey towns they are sometimes at less than 10 per cent and the average for the state is given as 28.5 per cent — all in defiance of the fact that the law has long required 100 per cent assessment.

With rates on land and improvement values what they are, it should be possible to exempt all improvements were land assessments raised to full value even on the present basis. Then, if it were possible to change the method of land assessment, making it cover the entire value, including the equity held by the taxing authority as well as that of the titleholder, it should be possible to abolish the iniquitous personal property tax. Would it not be possible to educate the people generally to see the wisdom of such a simplification of their tax laws? We believe that conditions in New Jersey are not very different from conditions generally: we know of one broad area in another state where assessments are generally at 10 per cent of true values.

There are some reasons why it might be wise to work on a county-wide or even a state-wide basis in New Jersey. There is a good deal of industry that is outside the cities, and there is no reason why benefits of reform should not be extended throughout the whole state. New Jersey is a densely settled state, excelled only by Rhode Island, often with little demarcation between municipalities, and it is more homogenous than many states. In this state there is reason to believe that many have been educated to the wisdom of what we propose. We believe that, if properly organized and handled, there would not be too much difficulty in putting through a program county by county. If assessments on site values were to be steadily raised over a period of ten or fifteen years, the way would be open for the complete change. We believe that all that is necessary is organized effort, well directed and aimed particularly at interesting and educating the general taxpaying public. Unquestionably were New Jersey to act in this way it would result in drawing both residents and industries from its two great neighboring states, New York and Pennsylvania.

Lessons from Other Cities

Conditions the country over are similar in principle although different in detail. An outstanding city is the nation's capital. From our figures, tax-exempt properties have generally been eliminated and in Washington the percentage of exempt property runs very high. The ratio of improvement values to land values is about 2.13 and the tax rate, notably low, is not much more than half of that in many cities. The government of the city is a federal function with little or no self-administered government. With the nation owning almost half of the city and paying most of the cost of its operation, it would be wise to go all the way, and we believe that there would be no hardship if it made the change all at once. This would make future acquisition of the needs of an ever-expanding government easier.

Washington is a city of tragic contrasts. It is one of the most beautiful cities in the world in some of its aspects, but parts of it are indescribably squalid and its alleys and slums are notorious. The housing situation is a national scandal, and we need have no fear of overbuilding for many a long year. With so low a tax rate land could easily carry a much heavier load with the much-needed buildings exempted, and owners of vacant lots and obsolete buildings would have every opportunity to protect themselves by improvement or by sale, for there is a lively demand. Even if the change were made in a single year little hardship would result: the tax rate on land values would be raised only a little higher than present rates in some cities where buildings are also taxed. Should it be necessary to spread the change over two or three years, the successive increases would scarcely be felt especially in these days when housing is imperatively needed. New and untaxed building and the consequent demand for lots would soon render the increased levy on sites negligible.

What political difficulties would be encountered in securing the necessary legislation cannot be foreseen, but the capital city would be a splendid example for all the nation. Slums and eyesores would be wiped out, housing conditions would be eased, acquisition of land by the nation facilitated, and Washington would be on its way to becoming what our capital city should be.

"Public" Housing and Slum Clearance

There would also be another great advantage in putting through this reform in the city of Washington. Such a demonstration, solving the twin problems of housing and slum clearance without expending any taxpayers' money, would be a very strong argument in Congress against the continued squandering of funds by the nation in housing developments.

We regard this intrusion of the federal government into local housing as utterly unconstitutional and, if anyone can find any clause in the Constitution which authorizes it, we should be glad to have it pointed out. There is certainly no sense in stretching "the general welfare" clause in an effort to make it cover the expenditure of the money of all the people for special benefits to favored groups in selected towns. Not only do we regard it as unconstitutional but we regard this policy as objectionable from every standpoint. It is totally unnecessary, as our congressmen would learn if they studied what has been done in Denmark; and, even if public funds were to be used in such ways, there is not the slightest excuse for the federal government putting up the money. It would be far better to have these follies committed by states and cities and counties than by the nation, for they can generally better afford it than can our insolvent Republic.

Another objection to public housing is that it is essentially communistic. It takes from some groups to give to others and from the people of the entire United States to give to favored states, all in complete harmony with Marx's principle of "from each according to his ability" and "unto each according to his needs," although the last clause is interpreted generally as spending according to political favor which can be won, for there is little question that the allotment of funds for housing is often influenced by attempts to win political support of doubtful states.

Incidentally, this work, like nearly everything which the government undertakes, is very badly done. Again and again we see the expenses so high that housing intended for the poorer classes costs far beyond their means, so often these plans utterly fail of their fulfillment and are flat failures. We think offhand of three, the Arthurdale scandal, which was finally worked out in a fairly satisfactory way but at a terrific cost, a local housing proposition financed in part with federal funds in the writer's home city, and the terribly wasteful and futile Quoddy experiment in Maine, abandoned as a failure. Another point which should not be forgotten is that all this public housing presents very unfair competition with private enterprise: some students say that we have not added anything to our housing by the expenditure of all this money, for they maintain that whatever was accomplished has been offset by decreased building by private enterprise. In any event, the total tax exemption of these public schemes increases the burden on owners of real estate, for what public housing does not pay in taxes they must make up: thus they must face the twofold injustice of illegitimate competition with their own properties and of having to pay for that illegitimate competition as well.

To illustrate the way public housing often operates, consider this example. The cost of forty-two state-aided housing projects in one recent year in one state amounted to over $34,000,000, an average of about $100 per month for each apartment. The average rental income was a shade under $42, leaving a deficit of $58 per month for each apartment, to be made up by a state subsidy of $8,000,000 and city subsidies of about $800,000, for which of course the taxpayers foot the bills. Tax exemption to these projects cost about $10,500,000 and this too came out of the pockets of the taxpayers, for the taxes which these projects did not pay had to be made up by private enterprise. The taxpayers paid $55.60 a month per apartment while the tenant paid only $42 a month.

Those benefiting by this subsidized housing were supposedly low-income families, with incomes under $4,500, which does not strike us as so very low. Furthermore, if the incomes of these families increased, as it often did, rent was not increased. Studies indicated that 15 per cent of those independently renting homes paid considerably less in rental for their own homes than they paid through taxes to subsidize more expensive homes of beneficiaries of public housing.

The man with little money is taxed to provide for others a better home than he can himself afford. The whole program is typical of the great fundamental evil of the abominable Marxian philosophy on which the whole program of public housing is based. Today we spend millions of dollars — in one state over ten million — on so-called public housing, funds for which are met very largely by owners of properties destined to suffer acutely by the unfair competition which these untaxed projects present to private enterprise. By a saner tax policy we would restore to the tax rolls the site values of all these public projects and do much to ease both the burden on the taxpayer and the unfair competition to which he is now subjected.

It is beyond the scope of this book to extend our study to cover many cities, but there are some points that may be gleaned from even a cursory investigation of a few.

Saint Paul, Minnesota, shows conditions doubtless duplicated in other cities. Land values declined about 25 per cent in ten years and actual shrinkage is even greater, for "not only has land decreased in value but many owners are unwilling to keep it . . . allowing it to revert . . . for taxes." Some years ago there were 18,751 forfeitures of vacant holdings and 334 properties with building values almost equal to site values and, on 59 holdings, buildings valued at more than the sites have been wrecked to cut tax costs. An office of land commissioners was established to operate and lease forfeited holdings, selling wherever possible, but only 2,200 parcels out of nearly 19,000 had been sold when we studied the city.

Buildings in that city declined in value about 12 per cent, and most of the new development takes place in suburban areas where population increase is far more rapid than in the city. It is significant, too, that while building values decline in the city, the number of holdings in nearby suburban towns, classified as improved, increased by almost 60 per cent in the last decade studied. Under a wiser plan enough of this growth would be centered in the city to save the situation and possibly outlying districts would seek annexation, to the advantage of all. Saint Paul is well managed and the area is prosperous, and it should be easier to make the change than where conditions are static or decadent.

We have gone into some detail regarding Saint Paul, for what went on there is duplicated elsewhere. All over the country many are moving into suburbs and getting away from the congestion of the city. Some of this movement is to be expected and is desirable, but many make such a move frankly to save taxes and to buy where land is cheap. The drift brings many difficulties to the city for its tax-base contracts and although, practically, the population of the city is increasing, this increase is not reflected in population figures or in tax receipts. To generalize about these conditions and trends is not easy, for we have no clear-cut definition of what is "suburban," but it is interesting to note that, despite decreasing population of some cities, what is called their "metropolitan area" often shows rapid growth.

Seattle shows conditions which are illuminating. In that city the law requires assessments on a 50 per cent basis but, while generally observed in the case of improvements, land assessments are often at about 25 per cent. The last time we looked it up land was assessed at something over $83,000,000 and improvements at about $125,000,000. Were the assessments equalized, total land values would be the higher and doubling the levy on sites and exempting all building values would give the city a greater revenue.

In the State of Washington they have perpetrated another folly. By constitutional amendment they limit the realty tax rate to 4 per cent, which, with improvements assessed on a 50 per cent basis and land often at 25 per cent despite the law, practically results in a rate of 2 per cent on improvements and 1 per cent on sites. This means low returns, and city deficits must be met by other taxes which bear most heavily on those of limited means. They have a 3 per cent sales tax and water rates have been increased by 50 per cent, not based on water costs but to meet general deficits.

Communism or Justice?

Our argument may involve recasting some habits of thought and it may give rise to questions. There are two lots, side by side and of the same dimensions, one vacant and the other occupied by a great skyscraper: would we tax them both alike? Yes, why not? The owners hold for personal advantage equal allotments of our common heritage and they are provided with the same services of government and facilities of society. It is true that one utilizes his and the other does not, but if you only scan the headlines of your morning paper while your neighbor reads his from start to finish, do you expect to pay less for your copy than he pays for his? The seller gives you both the same value and it is no concern of his what use you make of it. It may be said that the great building makes more demand on such public services as streets, sewers and transit systems; but, on the other hand, it offers far less hazard to the city, in disease, fire and crime, than does the old rookery or the vacant lot harboring ragweed, mosquitoes and nuisances.

But presumably the skyscraper yields a good income while the vacant lot yields nothing but tax bills: how does equal taxation square with the commonly accepted doctrine of "taxation according to ability to pay"? If one refuses to benefit by what is provided for him, that is his lookout and, with land taxed and improvements untaxed, it will certainly pay to put land to adequate use. As for "taxation according to ability to pay," or, as Karl Marx put it, "from each according to his ability," the writer is not a good enough communist to accept that dictum! It is fallacious and unethical — a principle which we flatly reject. It is nothing but extortion, taking what we can get wherever we can get it, exacting by *force majeure* of the state without a thought of justice or of right. If we mail a letter, the stamp costs three cents, whether bought by the mink-coated or the flannel-shirted. Why should not the services of the city be sold on the same equitable basis?

The objection is sometimes raised that "big business" will profit by the change. It will, but so will little business and the residents of the city. The temper of the times is to lay as heavy a charge as possible on corporations, particularly those in the utilities field, but we must deal justly with all, and whatever strengthens industry will increase our general prosperity, create employment and benefit all. The utilities do much for the city. A large part of the benefits received will be passed on to employees and consumers and, if the companies profit unduly, Uncle Sam's income tax man and state authorities will take care of that! No city can afford to overtax business or services essential to our common life.

In one town, dependent upon a single great corporation, effort is made to saddle as heavy a tax as possible on that company, and the city is beginning to pay dearly for its shortsighted oppression. Until defense brought a transient boom, the city was losing population very fast. The dominant company is establishing plants in other cities, and if the hometown does not watch its step it may again slip into the doldrums it experienced for many decades prior to the establishment of its great industry.

Another instance of dealing oppressively with a corporation comes to mind. A great and prosperous company employing many is located in a city where political conditions are a scandal and taxes ruinous. Founded on the proverbial shoestring, this company has grown phenomenally. The executives and many workers own their own homes and the management has long been noted for fair dealing, liberality and public spirit. But they are considering removal to another state, where taxes will be but a fraction of what they now pay, even though the move will cost them dearly in the sacrifice of realty. The city is advertising to attract new industries, but meanwhile it continues to drive away long-established concerns. Does this make sense?

Who Would Pay the City's Bills?

It is sometimes said that it is not right that those who own no land should pay no city taxes. But nobody would pay taxes. The city would support itself from its own earnings. One reader of the manuscript says it makes little difference whether we call what the city collects taxes or ground rent, for it is all the same to its people. Is this distinction a mere quibble?

As has been pointed out, what a tenant pays and loosely calls "rent" consists of (1) true rent for the site and (2) interest on the building and comparable improvements. Clearly, if the house it not taxed, the tenant will be relieved very materially. As for the true rent, that, as we have seen, is unchanged: the tenant pays what he now pays, but the landlord passes the ground rent on to the city, as is just and right. The tenant, then, unquestionably pays no tax.

The case of the owner-occupant is no different. He is wholly freed of taxes on the house but, instead of making only a partial payment to the city for benefits and services enjoyed, he settles this bill in full. Such a payment for values directly received is no more a tax than is, say, payment for postage stamps. Furthermore, the increase in the ground rent which he pays will be less than the taxes he has been paying on the building, provided he puts his land to adequate use.

Land is the first essential of life, labor and even of death. We must all have it and we must all use it — even the chap who disclaimed all interest in land because he lived on the third floor and worked on a ferryboat — and, since it differs in desirability, it is only fair that those who hold the most of it or the best of it should compensate the rest of us for the advantages which they enjoy. This really is the sum and substance of our case: instead of confiscating what is justly private property for the support of our city, we would support our common needs by collecting an equalization payment which would restore to all the people a just sharing of what the Creator has given to all and of values and services provided by our common life.

Taxing the Vacant Lot

The justice of imposing certain charges on the vacant lot is sometimes questioned. A vacant lot cannot be carried off by burglars; it will not burn up; it does not walk the pavement, ride in the subway or go to school. Why, then, should it pay to provide services which it cannot use? The answer is clear if we remember that these things, whether used or not, increase its value. We foolishly prohibit, by taxation of buildings, the utilization of these services and thereby impair their value, but nevertheless the owner reaps a benefit and often, as in the case of the subway, a very great benefit. Try to buy the lot once offered when all was a wilderness, after the city has expended millions in the conveniences of civilized living. Does the owner tell the purchaser that these services are worth nothing and hold his price down accordingly? He does not! He jacks the price up to several times what he would have been glad to take, and we pay a second time for what we have already bought with our taxes. We may all enjoy the parks, read in the libraries, visit the museum, send our children to the public schools and listen to band concerts in the square, *but we pay for what we get, not once, but twice.* Sympathize with the vacant lot owner because by prohibitive taxes we ban utilization of many services provided; but, remember, the empty lot produces nothing, consumes nothing, houses no one, employs no one and does nothing but hold back progress and swell living costs. Let the owner put his lot to profitable use and he too will gain.

Overbuilding and Zoning

It is sometimes feared that this program would lead to overbuilding. Is it always wise to encourage construction in congested sections where there is more need for elbow room, breathing spaces and parking lots? The fact that people live, work and die in such areas indicates a demand, and if they are determined to stay there they should be decently housed. Many would seek homes in less congested areas and, with speculative prices deflated and with freedom to build, there would be a drift away from the old rabbit warrens. Should this result in decreased ground rents in blighted sections, the enhancement of values in newer areas would more than offset any loss in city revenues. Another factor, too, would add to the attractiveness of less central locations. We have seen how improved transit increases ground rents and, were the city to recapture these values which it creates, transit would be better and cheaper and fares might no longer be a problem. If the real need is for open spaces and wider and straighter streets, the remedy is city planning. The reform proposed, coupled with excess condemnation, would facilitate the acquisition of necessary land, and sound public improvements could be made on a self-liquidating or even on a profitable basis. Those who would sell would gain and those who could afford to build wisely would be vastly bettered.

Men will always err in judgment and make mistakes and we have no starry-eyed scheme for making everything foolproof, but demand for housing, both residential and commercial, is almost limitless. There is a backlog of some two million homes, badly needed but not built, and the call for new homes and the replacement of old is set at about a million a year. Ten million home units are today said to be below standard. Remember, too, that our population is increasing rapidly. Both marriage and birth rates are rising; old people live longer and families are larger. To meet this demand on a basis satisfactory to builders and tenants alike is today impossible, but, with profits to builders increased and with "rents" reduced, opportunity is boundless.

But will there not be a temptation to build too high and to cover too much of the site, sacrificing yards, light and air? City planning and zoning may be necessary as they are today — require setbacks, restrict the proportion of the lot that may be built upon and the building height — but these problems will be far simpler. The proposed program will encourage a better-balanced growth in our cities. Avoiding congestion, and the deflation of speculatively inflated land prices, will make sites more readily available and at lower cost. In some cities there is abominable crowding with the building up of alleys, rear lots and areas which should have been kept open — all a flagrant cause of slums. Lower land prices and decentralization will more than offset any urge to crowd too much building on a lot.

Some controls may long be necessary, but the problem will be eased and not aggravated. Buildings of excessive height often destroy more land value than they create, supplying space beyond that justified by demand and shutting in the older and smaller structures. Better-balanced development will distribute land values more uniformly. Fifty- and hundred-story structures will be fewer, but the old two- and three-story rookeries which surround them will give way to buildings consistent with needs, say of eight or ten stories, and these will kill the demand for overpowering monstrosities.

Zoning, a point sometimes raised, is irrelevant to questions of taxation. How would we prevent the slaughterhouse from operating in a residential district or prevent a dance hall from opening next to a church or a school? We have no cure-all: the answer is zoning ordinances as at present, regulating the character and use of buildings in various sections. The problem would remain, but it would be simplified. Is it not probable that the higher cost of holding land idle or ill-used would promote usage in keeping with neighborhood needs? Today there is little to prevent the perpetuation of old and out-of-keeping buildings where they are not wanted, for, if replaced with better ones, the tax bill goes up. With improvements untaxed, many a slum building would give place to desirable construction and unwanted neighbors would drift to localities where lower ground rents testify to their probably being less of an annoyance.

The "Poor Widow"

Always we get the time-worn question of the poor widow's little cottage in a great business neighborhood or among more pretentious mansions. Would it not be hard on her to give up the old home with years of treasured memories? But how often do such situations arise? Do many impoverished widows live next door to great banks, hotels and apartment houses or in the shadow of palatial homes? Generally the "poor widow" makes a pretty good thing out of it by selling the old homestead at a high price and garnering a substantial "unearned increment." Under any plan there will be isolated cases of individuals having to do what they would not choose to do, but this is no problem in comparison to the hardships of today. Is there any reason why a valuable site, capable of serving many, should be monopolized by a single resident or by a trivial business, at the expense of the welfare and progress of all, unless adequate compensation is made for what the city gives? And the poor widow could sell more readily, and at a better price, were the untaxing of improvements to create a demand for her property.

Would Forfeitures Be Increased?

How can vacant land or obsolete and decadent buildings stand any increase in tax bills? Would not hardship result to many already in trouble, increasing delinquencies, forfeitures and losses, thereby cutting city revenues? In some very few cases this may result, but more often both owner and city will gain, by the restoration of value to site through building exemption.

Where there is an absurd excess of vacant lots, resulting from speculation and premature subdivision, the same forces will operate. We have cited the $6,000 house on the $400 lot and have shown how the owner would gain, and the same factors which benefit him would operate to give to the surrounding lots added value now being lost. Many would be built upon, and values would be restored to owners and on tax books. Where cities are caught in an orgy of speculation, many lots will be lost in any event, but how can this be prevented with speculation and subdivision so far in excess of any possible demand? Today there is no hope whatever, but, with buildings untaxed, new industries and residents will be attracted. There will be demand for sites, and some of the harm of unwise subdivision may be averted. Can things be much worse than they are today for these unfortunate land gamblers?

A Problem City

Illustrative of the difficulties encountered is the case of a city of some 20,000, detailed in a letter to the writer. The little town is in a bad way. "Small industry is going out, leaving shell holes and dumps, with abandoned factories and vacant real estate all around." Our correspondent says that there is only one substantial taxpayer left, and most of his tax is on the building and not on the site. What would happen to such a town?

The picture is not very reassuring, but what will happen if conditions are unchecked? Shall the town continue at the mercy of a single taxpayer? Why is "small industry going out?" To answer these questions requires a knowledge of the town which we do not possess, but our guess would be that things in this little city are comparable to those found in many a city. We know of a great metropolis which is sliding downhill fast for the simple reason that it is taxing industry to death. A small business was started in that city on limited capital, but it grew and prospered. Production, sales, employment and gross profits steadily increased, but taxes more than kept pace with expansion and net profits were not materially greater when thousands were employed than when the business was born with half a dozen workers. Recently the business just folded up; the owner was tired of "working to pay taxes," as he put it. And in the same city, another and very much larger business is today planning to move to another state, to cut tax costs and for no other reason whatever. Is it not possible that the same unfortunate forces have played their part in bringing disaster to the smaller city?

We can hardly believe that things are quite as bad as they are pictured by our correspondent. The little city is within ten miles of a great seaport metropolis, in a section where other towns are flourishing, and even it shows some growth. Were the change advocated spread over a dozen years, much land value would be restored. Industrial life might again pick up and suburbanites now locating in other centers would have inducement to build and to live there. We do not know local conditions but hazard a guess that, if things are as bad as described, decadence will continue unless something is done. Is it not better to take some chances rather than to let the little city go to destruction without an effort to save it?

Who Loses?

It is hard to have much patience with one objection sometimes raised. It is occasionally argued that somebody must lose, for one man's gain is always another's loss. Thank God our lives are planned on no such vicious philosophy. In no Pollyanna spirit of sentimentality, but just as hard, commonsense and cold-blooded reasoning, we must see that we all share and depend upon each other's prosperity. If we had the wit to grasp this simple truth there would soon be an end to much shortsighted selfishness.

In the long run we cannot possible live or thrive by swindling one another. If the shoemaker and the tailor trade their products, each must gain or the loser will quit; production of one commodity will halt, trade will stop, and no one will profit. To continue to benefit by specialization of skills, mass production and the division of labor, both must profit. Life should never be a game of privilege, of exploitation or of taking advantage, and what is proposed will bring benefit to all, excepting only those who seek to harvest where others sow. Don't be confused by fallacious argument based on the unsound premise that for one to gain another must lose.

Assessments and Corruption

Even aside from the fallacy of today's assessment theories already discussed, there is much that is wrong in the administration of our present follies. Methods and practices vary widely, as evidenced by recourse to equalization rates, and comparisons between cities mean little unless assessments and tax rates are taken in conjunction with one another. The assessors' oath "to assess all properties fairly, impartially and at true sales value" is a dead letter, for assessments are often frankly made at a definite percentage of that figure and sometimes at several times the market value.

There is scarcely a city where politics does not play a part in assessment, and often taxation is seen as an instrument in the hands of a dominant party to curry favor and influence votes. In one city, officials tell protesting owners to learn to "vote right" before airing their grievances, and the first move is to win the support of the ward leader. As this is written we have a story of political henchmen seeking to buy a property at far less than its worth and threatening that, were the offer refused, increased assessment would force a sale. The owner, a poor woman unable to secure redress, refused the offer and, apparently the threat was carried out.

The change advocated would go far to remedy these conditions. Taxation of buildings opens the way not only to corruption but to honest errors, for, even with the best intentions, it is difficult to appraise buildings with accuracy. One house is larger, but the smaller is newer and better built; one has a slate roof, but the shingled house has one more bath; one is insulated, but the other has a better heating system. It is almost impossible to agree on relative values, and a gorgeous opportunity is open to political skulduggery.

There is another phase of this question too. A comparatively new six-story building stood on a valuable lot. It was taxed at a substantial figure, and properly so if we accept the present system. Long before the building showed any deterioration it was torn down to make way for a building three times as high. The old building, modern, fireproof and fully rented, certainly could not be said to be worthless but, when razed, its value was less than demolition costs. How is such a building to be assessed, even with the best of intentions? It might be said to be worth several hundred thousand dollars or it might be held to be utterly valueless, and politically minded officials could justify either position. Remember the Belmont Hotel in New York City? What was that first-class modern building worth for the last few years before it was razed to cut tax bills?

With taxation of buildings ended, we would get rid of these difficulties so conducive to corruption. Assessing only sites leaves far less opportunity for error, and discrimination is too obvious to be condoned. Two lots, side by side and of the same dimensions, cannot be differently appraised, though one be owned by a Republican and the other by a Democrat. Land can be seen, measured and valued by anyone, and tax books will be purged of fraud, error and favoritism, and this is notably true of urban land, which seldom contains concealed improvements such as artificially produced fertility or drain tiles. The veriest tyro can judge its value better than the expert can appraise the building, its contents or what is concealed in a safe-deposit box, and experience has demonstrated the difficulty of even defining income in a fair and satisfactory way. There are systems of land valuation almost scientifically exact, taking into account street character, exposure, proximity to other streets and corners, transit facilities and nearly every factor. By assessing only ground rents, the problems of assessment would be made simple and many evils and injustices would vanish.

A minor complication may arise from the fact that some municipal improvements have been paid for by property owners through special assessments and therefore belong, in equity, to them and not to the city; but these charges seldom include such greater items as reservoirs, main trunk lines, filtration and sewage-reduction plants and similar major costs. The city, therefore, has some equity and generally it bears the expenses of upkeep and operation. Except where such special assessments are comparatively recent, property owners have generally been compensated by years of service.

To meet the problem of recent assessment of such charges, a deduction might be made from ground rents for some years and all unpaid charges of this character remitted. By such course, the city will virtually repurchase these investments, and future outlays should be met by the city. Expenditure should be regarded as capital investment, to bring return in higher future ground rents, justified by services rendered and higher value of tenure. This will reduce delinquency and forfeiture, and frequently sudden, and sometimes heavy, assessment of such costs brings real trouble. In Saint Paul many fine homesites with all local city improvements were forfeited "because too large a share of the costs was assessed" against the properties. The city lost not only normal taxes but special assessment as well, resulting in a deficit in their improvement fund of nearly $4,000,000. Had the city met these improvement costs and exempted all buildings, most of these lots would have been saved to the owners and would have paid ground rents in increasing volume.

Peace and the Post-war Problem

When this book was originally written we were plunged in war. Today we are at peace, if you can call it peace. Nevertheless, all the world is in revolution and we speak now not of armed conflict but of upheaval in habits of thought and ways of life and of justice and even of religion. We ask "why," no longer content to take things for granted. Great majorities overseas have accepted a political philosophy supported, until recently, by only a small and discredited minority. In America we travel much the same path. As John T. Flynn has shown in his excellent book, *The Road Ahead*, the greatest danger of communism to America may be not in the communism as it exists abroad but as it is making rapid headway right here at home while the American public sits back indifferent and ignorant of what is going on before our very eyes.

Discussion of the wisdom of these changes is apart from present purposes, and this has been treated by the writer in other pages. What we now emphasize is the inevitability of change: like it or not, the world of tomorrow will be very different from the world of yesterday. To oppose all change is futile, and our task must be to guide it into safe and beneficent channels.

Too often we fall prey to an indolent habit of seeking to escape thought by recourse to names and labels. The word "radical" connotes a crank who would throw overboard much which has proved its worth, but the true radical is not one who uproots the flowers with the weeds but one who goes to the root of every question. "Conservative," sometimes the brand of the stand-patter, more correctly means one who "holds fast to that which is good," accepting only change which gives promise, and "liberal" should mark those who seek all righteous liberty, not extremists and fanatics.

Thought is the first prerequisite to action, and it is the first duty of every man to think without prejudice, not content with tags and slogans. What is proposed in this book is radical, for it goes to the roots of the preservation of our rights, but it is far more conservative than present tax policies, which take regardless of justice. It is liberal in that it will give a larger measure of liberty, restoring much that is destroyed today and providing broader opportunity, easing those conditions which foment restlessness, discontent and rebellion and which naturally promote an urge for immoral, unjust and disastrous socialism or communism. Relieve the pressure of excessive taxation and open the door to the progress of industry, to thrift and the resumption of personal responsibility. Protect everyone of us in our full rights to property, whether it be personal property in the product of life and labor, which justly belongs to the individual, or a communal right to a just sharing in the benefits resulting in the values given to a common heritage by the common life by our government.

All these aims — and can anyone question their validity? — will be promoted by the program which we propose. Indeed, we can go further and say that *they can never be achieved without acceptance of this program.* We do not offer a cure-all for all of man's ills or for every social evil, but we do say that until the changes which we recommend are made it will be impossible to have social justice. All civilization rests upon the sanctity of property. Underlying the foundation of this country, with its profession of a faith in the natural rights of man to life, liberty and the pursuit of happiness, lies an assertion of the right of the individual to what he produces by his labor, and the only way that this can be achieved and insured is through the program which we propose. This, the collection of the income resulting from the values which our common life gives to our common inheritance from the Creator, is the only means by which we can support government other than by the seizure of personal property.

Today industry struggles under a crushing load of taxation, and this burden will become increasingly oppressive in days ahead. Already we approach the proverbial last straw, and industry may be literally taxed to death. Some imagine that taxes can be levied only on men of wealth and on "big business," but our lives and interests are so intertwined that no group can suffer alone. In a world of contracting industry it will be the job-seeker who suffers first, and we cannot oppress those who give employment without injury to those who seek it. It is to private enterprise and free industry that we must look to take up the slack. It is futile to look to public employment, hoping to provide wages for "boondoggling" by borrowing from one another. Make our public undertakings self-supporting and profitable, and it will be quite another matter: then public employment will become possible and sound.

Our Social Responsibility

A sound and stable continuation of building activities will go far to give employment through the whole chain of industry and it will do much to re-establish business on a firm foundation. It will give relief to productive industry, no longer mulcted of a large part of its earnings to support local government. It will solve the problem of housing and rid our cities of festering slums. The city alone cannot meet every difficulty, but we deal here only with the city problem, and that in itself is vital. Considerably more than half of our people live in the cities, and on them the farmer is dependent. Setting our own house in order will make a good start and, as a practical matter, it is easier to bring those of a city to a wise course of action than to induce many millions to think and to act.

Not one of us can escape a share in the guilt of today. We permit — we encourage — the monopolization of a common birthright and of a common product; we deny to the worker — and that means

[81]

the executive and the thinker as well as the laborer—the full reward of this toil; we encourage idleness and speculation and discourage production, and all mankind suffers. The American people are at heart fair and generous; it is a question of blindness and not of selfish depravity, but fools often work quite as much harm as do knaves. Our blindness is the result of indifference, mental inertia and willingness to accept, without thought, traditions and usages which hark back to feudalism.

No one with a conscience can view complacently things as they were in even the best of times, when many of our people lived on the very edge of mere animal existence. For generations we were a young country, blessed as was no other land with opportunity which appeared limitless. A great free frontier lay open to all, and that was the secret of much of our growth and progress. But that day is gone forever, and each year we approach more closely to the problems and difficulties of older lands.

We speak for no group and for no class. The landowner is no more to be blamed than are the rest of us: he plays the game by rules made and accepted by all and he, too, often suffers. We preach no "class-consciousness" and still less do we condemn the wealthy, "Wall Street" or any imaginary hobgoblin of the "trusts." Our only plea is to protect every man, rich or poor, in rights which are his—the individual right to his own earnings and a share in a common heritage to which value is given by the common life.

Objection may be raised to the proposals offered on the ground that, by moving too fast, changes will be drastic and hard. We might make the change more gradually, but the problem of city financing, already acute, calls loudly for relief. In normal times we might stretch the change over longer periods, but times are far from normal and delay is dangerous. We cannot afford to be caught doing "too little and too late." Unless we do something and do it quickly, disaster will be upon us, and it can come through our own folly quite as readily as by alien aggression. Listen to Macaulay's warning to America of almost a century ago:

"I cannot help foreboding the worst . . . Your government will never be able to restrain a distressed and discontented majority. Either some Caesar or Napoleon will seize the reins of government with a strong hand or your republic will be as fearfully plundered and laid waste by barbarians in the twentieth century as the Roman Empire was in the fifth; with this difference, that the Huns and Vandals who ravaged the Roman Empire came from without, and that your Huns and Vandals will have been engendered within your own country by your own institutions."

The Dangers of Centralization

With the increasing tendency to ignore the Constitution and to permit the federal government to usurp the functions, responsibilities and the privileges of the state and of local divisions of government, the future looks ominous. Tax rates go up, as does our bonded indebtedness, inflation continues to increase, buildings and industries are saddled with an ever-growing burden. What will happen to the finances of our cities? Facing a crisis and in frantic effort to escape, they resort to a dangerous expedient and seek to transfer their responsibilities to state and nation. They clamor for subsidies for this and that, but the difficulty can never be eased in that way. By whatever agency our taxes are levied, we ourselves must keep filled the pork barrel from which we would grab and, by and large, the taxpayers lose more from subsidies than they gain. All such schemes are open to another grave objection: he who pays the piper calls the tune, and trying to shoulder off onto state or nation obligations which are ours means the loss of self-government and the destruction of our liberties. We clamor for subsidies for schools, roads, public improvements, housing, the relief of destitution and for many a supposed benefit, and for this mess of pottage — and a mess it is! — we sell our freedom. Remember Franklin's warning: "They who can give up essential liberty, to obtain a little temporary safety, deserve neither liberty nor safety."

Tax Delinquency and Forfeiture

The problems of delinquency and forfeiture will be eased, but they must still be faced and it is not improbable that they may be aggravated. What shall be done with realty on which taxes remain unpaid?

Taxes constitute a lien collectible by seizure in one way or another, but legal formalities are complex and so costly that it is often impossible for a city to secure clear title by any reasonable procedure in any reasonable time. For years rights of redemption are vested in former owners and, even if seldom exercised, title is cluttered and neither city nor purchaser can secure unquestioned ownership. The usual process of foreclosure is frequently of little avail, involving costs scarcely justified in the case of small undeveloped parcels of low value. A simple measure sometimes adopted will help: provide for foreclosure "in rem," as the lawyer puts it, instead of "in personam," doing away with the necessity of hunting up and serving all individuals concerned and proceeding against the property instead of against all who may possess a shadow of a claim.

The problem of forfeitures is primarily a problem of vacant lands.

[83]

In Dearborn, Michigan, of 4,000 lots, 3,000 were vacant and 1,240 were tax-delinquent in 1930, but ten years later this number had increased to 2,600. In one town in western New York tax arrears on over 22,000 vacant lots make up over 96 per cent of total unpaid taxes. In Saint Paul, although there has been delinquency even in the heart of the city, with substantial and well-located buildings forfeited, the city has acquired 18,000 vacant lots against 334 improved parcels; and in Jamestown, New York, of the 4,000 parcels acquired through non-payment of taxes, only 120 are improved. The magnitude of the problem is illustrated by nine cities where the total of accrued and unpaid taxes exceeds the amount of annual collections.

All this means expense in assessing and handling worthless claims. One city sets the cost of assessment at $1.70 a year for each parcel, accounting at $1.20 more, and in a single year the cost of advertising tax sales has been as high as $14,000. In at least one state, cities must also meet another obligation: each municipality must pay all state and county taxes on realty even though the city is unable to collect. Every city faces these problems in one form or another, and every unpaid tax bill increases what others must pay, so things go from bad to worse and the disastrous process rolls up like a snowball.

A Problem of Clouded Titles

Sometimes non-payment brings little result except abandonment, with title so clouded that it is not worth the effort to clear it. Mr. Philip H. Cornick tells of a subdivision in which lots were given away as premiums with boxes of soap. On one such lot, of which the deed was recorded a half century ago, no taxes have ever been paid. Who owns the lot today? It is Mr. Cornick's guess that the original owner has long since been gathered to his fathers, the estate distributed under a will in which this most doubtful asset was not mentioned, and whatever claim remains is lost and scattered among scores of descendants. Meantime, unpaid taxes and penalties have piled up, amounting to more than seven times the assessed value. True, the lot may be worth nothing in itself, but there are hundreds, if not thousands, of such parcels. A simple and inexpensive procedure should be established by which the city can take clear title, for no one profits with things as they are. It may seem to matter little what becomes of such holdings, but, with improvements untaxed, they would often acquire some value and would justify the payment of ground rent in many a case. If, however, this is utterly hopeless, such lots in the aggregate may have considerable value if consolidated and the harm of foolish subdivision undone. Even isolated lots are sometimes useful for widening and straightening of streets, and often it is possible to effect desirable exchange.

[84]

Another similar instance has recently been reported. A toll bridge was built many years ago across the Mohawk River at Schenectady and, for some reason unknown to us, it was provided that all owners across the river were to be guaranteed free passage of the bridge in perpetuity. Some bright chap saw possibilities in this provision and, acquiring a bit of more or less wasteland, cut it up into divisions, each of only a square inch or two. These, constituting ownership of realty and providing a permanent bridge pass, found a ready sale. The years have passed and the old toll bridge has given way to a new free bridge, so ownership of these little scraps of land is worthless. Many of the deeds were never recorded and are forgotten, and of course taxes have gone unpaid and no title can be traced. Today nothing can be done to clear title and the tract is utterly worthless. We believe, however, that these evils have been largely abated by legislation in recent years in many states.

Such land may have possibilities for community uses — parks, playgrounds, boulevards and "green belts." One city has developed a park which, through resulting increment in values of surrounding property, will more than reimburse it for lost taxes. In another, reverted holdings provide a playground, and, in still a third, a small pond gives the people a winter skating rink. Many cities in Europe and a few in America have established municipal forests or nurseries to provide plants for parks and boulevards. Land in crowded, neglected slum areas may provide parking lots or playgrounds and serve for municipal garages or storage.

Some Simple Reforms

Simplify the way in which title to delinquent holdings can be taken and then, instead of trying to force profitless or impossible sales, let the city hold such properties, leasing for ground rent, with all improvements, past or future, exempt. The best way to fix rent on holdings of uncertain value would be by auction of long-term leases, taking bids in terms of annual rent, readjusted at intervals according to changing conditions. Titles would be kept clean, income restored to the city, demoralization of realty values ended, and many a holder now wiped out would retain and improve his property. In one city 80 per cent of vacant lots acquired by forfeiture have been improved when sold after artificial inflated values were deflated, showing what might be done were improvements untaxed. Some similar course may be worth consideration by the small, decadent city now relying on the single taxpayer.

It is possible that such procedure might place those who continue to pay taxes at a disadvantage, encouraging non-payment. To obviate this and to expedite the collection of ground rent instead of taxes, permit any owner so electing to deed his property to the city for a nominal payment, retaining tenure and thereafter paying only full ground rent. Then he can build the home so long desired, incurring no added levy, and city revenues will be assured. Don't say that such a transfer and public ownership is "communistic." Final title is already lodged in the state by the Constitution, and what we propose is only the recognition and legalization of what already exists.

Under existing laws, cities seldom have the right to buy, hold or lease realty for purposes other than actual public use. The rights of the city should be broadened to permit such undertakings. There is sometimes provision for what is called excess condemnation, giving city or state the right to acquire land beyond that directly needed, in order that it may reap the return from public improvements. Such legislation, however, is often obscure and forgotten, and excess condemnation is exercised far less often than it should be. We can learn from European experience where cities are often far more progressive than American municipalities. The opening of the famous Avenue de l'Opéra in Paris cost the city some $11,000,000, but by the sale of benefited land, acquired by excess condemnation, it realized a profit of almost six times the cost of the new street — another instance of the increase in land values by public improvements. Excess condemnation may be of minor importance if the city recovers in higher ground rent the greater revenue resulting from improvements, but there are practical aspects not to be ignored. Sometimes the opening of new streets, or the widening and straightening of old, leaves property owners with small, misshapen remnants of little or no value. What good is a long wedge of land five feet wide at one end and a few inches wide at the other? About all it is good for is a billboard, and this injures surrounding values. Of course there is a vociferous objection to proposed improvements which leave property owners with such worthless scraps of land, and sometimes they recover in damages more than would have been the cost of purchasing the entire parcel under excess condemnation.

A complete overhauling of present procedure would overcome many evils and end many hardships. Consider the case of a famous hotel in one of our great cities. For years it has been unable to earn its taxes, high because of the levy on the very valuable building. No taxes whatever are paid and the city is powerless to act. If a tax sale is forced, there will be few bidders, for the hotel is well operated and has a good name and new management could do no better with it than the present owners. The city would gain nothing and would suffer from the closing of its famous hostelry, especially as the cause of the jam became known. Tax conditions in both city and state are notorious, and they can ill afford to add to discontent and unrest. There is little question that, were the property offered on lease for ground rent, the owners would re-establish things on a profitable footing and the tax yield, while theoretically less than is charged today, would actually be far more than the nothing now being collected.

When the Florida boom collapsed it brought ruin to many, and financial chaos was widespread. Many governmental units were in default — 47 counties out of 67; 165 municipalities out of 289; 204 school districts out of 882 — and, since many units overlapped, the difficulties of many districts and counties involved the cities. To clean up the situation, bonds, purchasable often at fifty cents on the dollar or even less, were made acceptable in payment of delinquent taxes, and this discrimination made it an object to let taxes accumulate. Delinquency still dragged, sometimes for many years, and finally payment for taxes for only a single year, and that made in depreciated bonds, would clear all arrearage. Were the cities to reform their policies, they could take title and, leasing for a fair ground rent with improvements exempt, many an owner, now dispossessed to the benefit of no one, might hold and improve his property instead of being wiped out.

This modification of present usage would save many an owner. We call to mind a delightful apartment house in a Florida city, offered to the writer at a sacrifice price but with a mass of unpaid tax liens. The owner would not have been forced almost to give away a potentially valuable property had the building been tax-free, and at least some tax revenue would have been collected by the city. Ground rents would have been willingly paid, the burden on other taxpayers eased, and the owner would have been safe in the possession of a property now lost.

Increased City Revenue

With building values no longer eaten into or destroyed by taxation, owners will gain enormously; but, since the value of a building is fixed primarily by replacement cost, we cannot look for enhancement beyond this point. Absolute increase of value will attach to sites and not to buildings, reacting to the benefit of the city; finances will be established on a sound basis and we may reasonably anticipate an ever-growing revenue, with many economies in city administration. The influence of social conditions on land values has been recognized for ages, even Cicero calling attention to it. Zangerle, in his book, *Real Estate Appraising*, quotes a suggestive passage from John B. Sharpe's *New Political Economy*:

"Those efforts at social amelioration . . . such as the promotion of temperance, the purification of politics, greater efficiency in moral and religious instruction, the heightening of the civic sense and the political judgment, every aspiration indeed for what is higher and better, every impulse toward what is good and noble that finds organized expression in society, serves but to increase the rental value of land . . . Imagine . . . a community in which all citizens were honest, temperate and industrious: in which vice and indolence and immorality were no longer to be found! Would not many persons eagerly seek homes in such a community? . . Is it not clear that it would find expression in increased rent, and that those who owned the land . . . would charge a premium for the use of it? Manifestly they would and . . . it becomes apparent that the economic effect of such reforms is not to increase wages . . . but to increase the value of land."

This may sound like the Elsie books and some may question if life in such a community would be very exciting, but the principle is sound. In a community of angels, none would endanger life or property; police would scarcely be needed; courts would be idle, prisons vacant, and calls for charity would be few. The schools would do their job in half the time, with half the expense, teaching infant paragons who would never play hooky, throw peanut shells on the streets, scribble on fences or break windows. Economies in city and private expenditures would be reflected in higher land values and ground rents, gladly paid. To reduce these complex factors to figures and formulas is impossible, but competent students see an almost certain probability of city income increasing far beyond what now seems possible.

It is sometimes argued that the proposed reform will open the way to extravagance and corruption, but the direct nature of the levy, doing away with the chicanery of indirect taxation, will curb and not aggravate these evils. It is as silly for a city to refuse to collect its rightful income as it would be for a man to refuse his pay envelope lest he use the contents unwisely. Every city could use profitably far more than it now collects, especially as such outlays will be profitable investments reflecting greater future income. There is not a city which would not be a better place in which to live and work, with good pavements, parks, playgrounds and cultural advantages.

Collection of present revenues by ground rents instead of by taxation has been emphasized, for this is the first step, but it is only a beginning. A constant budget has been assumed and we have considered only changing the method of its collection. This, in itself, will not increase the city revenue, but collection will be easier, cheaper and surer. But, having gone this far, *we should then go all the way and collect for common needs all the income which justly belongs to the city, and this can be done without the slightest hardship or injustice, for property owners will reap the benefits from the use of these funds.*

[88]

How to Use This Surplus

The increased revenue might well be absorbed in part by remission of other municipal taxes, oppressive to industry and to the well-being of the people. The personal property tax, shown by long years of experience to be incapable of impartial imposition or collection, should be abolished if only in the interest of fair play. Particularly objectionable is the taxing of so-called intangibles — things in themselves of no intrinsic value, serving only as evidence of ownership of things already taxed. The factory is taxed in ways innumerable but, if the business is incorporated, the stock is again taxed in many states and cities, subjecting the same property to double or triple taxation. To tax both the property and vouchers for it is as unjust as it would be to tax a man on his watch, as some states and cities attempt to do, and then tax again the check which the repair man gives him for it. The man who owns his house free and clear is taxed once but, if unfortunate enough to have a mortgage on it, he is taxed in some states also on that lien, again double taxation, and particularly odious because it falls on the debtor class.

The sales tax falls in much the same category as a tax on buildings. It is a tax on enterprise and free exchange, upon which our prosperity rests, and it falls the hardest on those already close to the margin of subsistence. The same objection applies to a tax, camouflaged as a license, on the conduct of a legitimate business or profession. Ultimately it is paid by the consumer, and again those of smallest means suffer the most. It operates precisely like the sales tax. Why in the world should the poor fellow with an aching tooth have his sufferings increased by higher charges resulting from the tax imposed on the practice of dentistry?

There are taxes which are primarily the exercise of police power, such as the dog tax to keep our canine population within bounds, or the tax on dance halls or pawnships. Perhaps potential nuisances should pay the costs of their supervision but, as revenue measures, it is hard to defend them.

Some taxes, city or otherwise, are open to argument, notably those imposed on the liquor traffic and on gambling. The principle is clear and clean-cut if we can agree on our premises. If such operations are desirable business undertakings, they should not be taxed; if they are immoral or even anti-social, they should not be tolerated because government "takes a cut in the swag." The difficulty is that we are not all of one mind on our premises, so logic falls down and the best we can do is to compromise as we do today.

After many objectionable levies have been abolished, there probably will remain a surplus and for it there are many uses. In some cities it may be wise to use it in reducing bonded indebtedness; but, with the city established on a solid footing, a reasonable debt need bring no more anxiety to either debtor or creditor than does a moderate funded debt of a thriving corporation. Beyond such material improvements as we have mentioned, there are many services which a city might render to its people, *were costs met with legitimate income and not by the exaction of taxation.*

The writer is no friend to communism in any of its forms and decries programs which take from some to give to others. Government should not be a charitable organization, doing for men what they should do for themselves and undermining character and self-reliance, nor should it be an instrument for the redistribution of what they earn by their toil. Increasingly we are taking from all — or, worse yet, from a few — to do things for and give things to favored classes, and this is the very substance of communism. We say nothing of this communistic practice as a voluntary way of personal life — that the writer has discussed in other pages — but, *as a political policy, compelled by the force majeure of the state, it is immoral and unjust.* To deal fairly with all, to show no discrimination, and to enforce justice with an even hand, is the paramount duty of the state.

But much as we decry the socialistic-communistic trend of the times, under whatever colors it may sail, expenditure of a common income for a common good — for the good of all and not of a few — is free from this taint. In one great city the hospitals verge on bankruptcy because of inadequate payment by the city for charity cases committed by the authorities. These payments — only about half of actual costs — mean heavy deficits which have to be made up by constant "drives" and by increased charges to paying patients. We take from the charitably disposed to pay expenses which could be met from city funds, were the city to collect its rightful income. Instead of making the fairly well-to-do pay for the unfortunate, the city might well reverse its policy and pay enough to cover not only the full costs of indigent patients but also a good part of hospital overhead, thus reducing the financial burden of sickness to all. Even those in good circumstances often carry a crushing burden when sickness is prolonged and, could the city afford it, we see no objection to free hospitalization for all, with no more stigma of "charity" than in the case of public education. Hospitalization is not much subject to abuse, even if free: no one wants unnecessary operations and most of us would rather be up and around than on our backs in a hospital. This is but one example of how a large municipal income could be wisely and justly used.

Lessons from Experience

Our argument has been in part theoretical, and questions will arise regarding experience in line with this proposal. In Denmark a plan shaped on easing the burden on improvements has been a success, and all observers agree that the tremendous advance of that enlightened little country was due almost wholly to land reform. Between 1932 and 1937, levies on land values increased about 50 per cent while taxes on improvements were cut by more than 40 per cent, with full exemption of houses up to $2,500. The results speak for themselves: the average number of dwellings built annually increased by 74 per cent in about eight years, and "the problem of how to make room for those without shelter has simply ceased to exist."

With this new construction, the number of old tenements razed each year has been multiplied by more than sixteen, and Miss Margaret Bateman says that "by taking ground rent for public use the slum problem has been eliminated in Copenhagen." Tenantry is estimated at only 5 per cent — a mere fraction of what it is with us — and a great feudal system of land tenure has given way to broad ownership of small holdings by the masses, with only 2 per cent of the farms exceeding 150 acres. These great gains are reflected in all the life of the people. The standard of living has advanced enormously; poverty is gone and, in their cultural and educational life, a progress has been made which is truly remarkable.

In New Zealand, Australia, the British colonies in Central Africa and in many scattered spots, progress has been made and the soundness of the principle demonstrated. Some Canadian cities for years levied all real estate taxation solely against land values, with general satisfaction. In the United States we have gone more slowly, but partial steps have been taken in many places.

Private Enterprise or "Public" Operations?

In some cities it has long been the practice to grant partial exemption to new enterprises, often in ways more or less extra-legal. The weakness of these discriminatory programs is that they are unjust to the already-established, putting them at a disadvantage. Surely those who anticipate housing needs should not be made to suffer by unfair competition with later entrants into the field. This applies also to the exemption of limited dividend and non-profit undertakings, raising taxes and making things more difficult for those who would meet housing needs on a clean-cut business basis. Thus they retard a lasting solution of the problem.

For decades now we have been hearing much about "the housing problem," but we fail to see that it all lies in our folly of penalizing those who supply us with that for which we clamor. We have spent and are still spending, literally billions, wrung from the taxpayers, to provide "public housing" — all totally unnecessary.

These housing projects follow the usual pattern of almost all governmental business — waste, extravagance, corruption and general futility. They are usually tax-free, paying not even ground rent into the public treasury. Thus they offer a double-barreled competition to independent building: first, competing unfairly with heavily taxed private enterprise, and second, increasing the cost of private housing, for untaxed public developments mean higher taxes on private property. It is also charged by competent students that these public operations add nothing to our housing for, by unfair competition and by the priority which they frequently enjoy in buying scarce materials, they discourage as much new housing as they create.

Political housing operations are characterized by the general futility of much socialistic enterprise. Construction, design and the general scheme are often of the worst: consider Arthurdale, the scandals of the Quoddy project and the short life of the Saint Mary's development in Albany. A frequent blunder is to indulge in ruinous extravagance, raising costs and rents so that the original purpose is thwarted by putting the new housing out of the reach of those whom it was expected to serve, forcing tenants out of twelve- to forty-dollar-a-month quarters to build accommodations for the hundred-dollar-or-more-a-month accommodations, thus adding to the troubles of the needy in order to give subsidized housing to those who could and should earn it for themselves and pay their own way. This problem of providing for the wrong classes is often met by subsidizing the development, thus giving far better habitations to many than they can expect or pay for, and taxing some to give to others — and this is the very heart of communism.

Such programs are often pictured as Christian sharing such as was enjoined by Christ, but we cannot make stealing, which would be wrong for the individual, right by doing it collectively through the tax collector. To give and to share are said to be Christian duties, but the obligation to give does not imply a right to take. Christianity does not justify a gunman in taking the wallet, from which perhaps the owner should voluntarily give much, nor does it justify a government using force to take from some what is justly theirs, to redistribute the loot according to the ideas of politicians.

Any such socialistic-communistic programs involve a vicious evil: they demoralize our people, leading them to demand that others shall earn for them what they refuse to earn for themselves. Again and again dreamy sentimentalists, demagogues and loose-thinking individuals of both sexes declare that everyone has a *right* to good, modern housing. We have no right to any housing which we do not earn, though we have a right of access to our share of the God-given planet on which we must live. These flabby-minded souls, who preach and teach that some have a right to demand that others labor to provide for them, do incalculable mischief.

This madness also demoralizes government. If a city is unwilling or unable to provide everything it desires to all its people who are indisposed to earn what they want, it demands subsidies from the states. Then the states, swamped with demands, run to Washington for national subsidies, and each division of government thus prostitutes itself to gain favor, votes and popular support. The final outcome is ruinous taxation, hopeless public debt, ever-growing inflation and, worst of all, a people and a government demoralized and corrupt.

The problem of housing could be easily solved by the simple program of untaxing the housing that we want and collecting the support of government in a way which will bring idle and inadequately used urban land onto the market, making it available to the would-be homeowner or home builder. Give private enterprise the green light and we will go ahead, without public subsidies, and build our own homes. Exempt housing, but not the land upon which it stands, and our housing problems will soon be solved, and without political scheming and robbing some to give to others, but in a sound and sensible businesslike way.

In many sections there is a dangerous contraction of the tax base as a result of the acquirement of broad acres by the federal government. How far this purchase of land has gone few realize, and one wonders if much of this purchasing power is not in direct violation of the Constiution, which authorizes the nation to buy land only for definite, specific uses, and then only "by consent of the legislature of the state in which the same shall be."

Attempt has been made to correct the injustice of paying no local taxes by what is called "in lieu" payments, but it is hard to see why the nation should not meet its just share of local government costs on the same basis as does the individual owner. Even in the case of city-owned realty — schools, firehouses and the like — though payment of taxes would mean taking from one pocket to put in the other, there would at least be the merit of putting accounting on a sound basis with costs allocated where they belong.

Any discrimination between various classes of property, between new industries and old, new housing and old, or between developments financed on different plans or from different sources, opens the door to many evils, especially when exercised in ways not quite legal and aboveboard. Often there is a time limit on exemption; at best the future is uncertain and always favoritism, politics and corruption play their part. Whatever we do should be done openly, legally, impartially and in a way as detached as possible from politics.

A Lesson from Pittsburgh

In 1913 Pittsburgh passed the so-called graded-tax law, providing for the progressive shift of municipal taxes from improvement values to land values in cities of the second class — namely, Pittsburgh and Scranton — until the city taxes on improvements were cut in half and the burden transferred to land values. For reasons which it is scarcely possible to discuss here, there have been complications in Scranton, owing largely to the fact that the city is built upon coal lands, which make it a less desirable "guinea pig" than its bigger sister city, where about three and a quarter millions of taxation have been transferred to land values. That the results are good is attested by almost every interest and class, including the Chamber of Commerce, the Board of Trade, the Civic Commission, leading business houses, innumerable labor unions and many representative groups. The Taxpayers' League reports that 95 per cent of all homeowners now pay lower taxes and, although the savings in dollars is greater in the case of great commercial buildings, "the home-owner stands out as the chief direct beneficiary and his savings in proportion are usually greater than those . . . of any other class." In a typical residential ward, out of a total of 3,272 owners of improved property, only twenty-two fail to show a saving and, in these cases, buildings are relatively of little value.

Although Pittsburgh has gone ostensibly halfway, actually they have covered but a small fraction of the road, for, by restrictions of state law, county and school taxes are not affected, and these combined almost equal the regular city levy. Furthermore, an unfortunate change in assessment has kept the valuations of sites unduly low and increased the assessments of buildings and thus has operated to counteract some of the benefit. Nevertheless, this beginning has proved the value of the plan and the soundness of the principle and has led to the enactment of the state law already referred to permitting similar changes in the third-class cities of the state.

We have no panacea. Man is fallible, often unconscionably stupid, and frequently selfish. These frailties will be with us until the Golden Age, but because some evils will long persist shall we close our eyes to a reform which will clear away many difficulties and make far easier the approach to others? For the broad principle advocated there is every argument, and it is this which we stress, suggesting only tentatively details of procedure and method.

A Program and a Formula

The first step for a city which would recapture what belongs to it and which seeks prosperity and not stagnation is to make a thorough study of its specific problem.

The examples of Albany and of New York suggest a method and formula generally applicable. Whether or not it is desired to include personal property as we have suggested in the state of New Jersey, or franchise values as we have suggested in New York City, is a matter for local consideration. The general principle is to divide the total of assessed values which we wish to exempt from taxation by the total of land valuations, and this gives the percentage of increase in ground rent required to counterbalance the exemptions. As we have pointed out, this increase in ground rent collected is best effected by increasing the assessments and, as we have attempted to show, this is perfectly just and fair. As a general policy, we would propose keeping the tax rate where it is, although if a city desires to increase its budget the rate might also be increased on land but not on buildings.

Initiative in making a study of the situation in any city may well be taken by some civic body such as the chamber of commerce, or, better, by a wider and more representative group, without necessarily any commitment until justified by findings and study. Funds will be required but no very great sum at the start and, when a definite program has been worked out and approved, effort should be made to enlist as many elements as possible to work for its acceptance. The keenest interest may be expected from those who will benefit most directly — the owners of improved property, whether modest homes or great buildings — and the many who suffer under the conditions of today. The principle has been approved by a special committee of the American Institute of Architects, and it should be easy to win the support of engineers, contractors, supply houses, and labor groups in construction and affiliated trades. Because of the effect on housing, those interested in this problem, and in its twin, slum-eradication, should be approached. The correlated economies in both public and private charity and the broad social aspects will appeal to many.

Interest and support of all directly concerned in real estate interests, and particularly brokers, should be enlisted, for they will benefit greatly. The opportunity to build, without any increase in the tax bill, should give impetus to the sale of sites, especially in blighted and slum areas where today, often, everything is going to rack and ruin. We have in mind a district in our own city where it is impossible to secure a mortgage on any terms because the neighborhood, once regarded as desirable, is slipping fast, values and rents falling steadily, property deteriorating and delinquent in taxes and often neglected and going to pieces. Yet this section is well located and would have possibilities were it not that crushing taxation makes building virtually an impossibility. In fact either rebuilding or proper maintenance is often impossible.

Under a saner general plan, or even under the optional plan suggested, making untaxed building possible, we believe that values in this section and many like it would be saved. Sales would again be possible and rebuilding, even if not new building, would do something to restore the neighborhood.

The city real estate operator or broker is almost wholly concerned with improved realty or with holdings about to be improved. He sometimes deals in vacant lots, in ramshackle slum buildings, firetraps and rookeries, and there are new subdivisions, but are not these properties generally traded in in the expectation of development and building? Once in a blue moon some penny-pinching speculator may buy something just to hold it indefinitely, until the growth of the city makes it possible to garner unearned increment, but this is rare and generally not very profitable to the broker. Do not most real estate deals fall into one of the following classes?

1. Rental, sale or management of good property for legitimate occupancy, either residential or commercial.

2. Sale of property cluttered by old obsolete buildings usually earning little, for the purpose of rebuilding or remodeling or displacing an old rattery with modern construction.

3. Sale of vacant land or purchase of subdivisions, and ultimately the resale of these new extensions into the outskirts. Are not these properties sold to those who intend to build?

4. Sometimes, in larger cities, negotiation of long-term ground leases as sites for great modern buildings. Are not such operations practically always with a view to immediate construction?

5. Secondary lines of writing insurance on buildings and negotiating mortgages, nearly always placed to provide funds for building or for reconstruction or improvement.

If these categories cover the bulk of the business of the real estate operator, do not his operations depend almost always on the improvement of property, either past or future? Will not any program which stabilizes the profits of building react to support and strengthen land values and benefit their business? Would not complete tax exemption of all buildings, past, present and future, increase their earnings and give stimulus to the improvement of the city?

Tenants should be educated to see that whatever reduces the cost of housing will reduce "rents," and bring substantial savings. This educational work may call for patience, for rent-payers are sometimes short-sighted and let animosity to landlords blind them to their true interests. The tenants in one great building, incensed by a raise in "rents," sent a committee to the city hall to "get back" at their landlord, demanding an increase in the assessment of the building on account of the greater rent roll. They accomplished their purpose, taxes were increased, and they themselves had to meet another jump in rents. Just one more instance of the passing on of taxes on buildings to tenants!

A more direct approach would be through the city fathers but experience shows that those whom we call leaders are more often followers, reacting to pressure of constituencies amd seldom themselves taking much initiative. We generally get what we want, or what we think we want, and there will be less difficulty and less resentment if the people themselves demand the change, instead of seeking its imposition by authority through the pressure of a few.

Some Questions of Legislation

Legislation, and perhaps constitutional amendment, will be necessary, but lobbying should not be undertaken prematurely without study of local conditions, some degree of public education and the formulation of a definite program. Into detailed questions of legislation we do not enter, for requirements are different in each state, and the writer has no training in the subtleties of law. It is believed that no national action would be required, except of course for the city of Washington, but state legislation will generally be necessary and it should be permissive and not mandatory. Home rule must be rigidly preserved, with each city free to follow its own lights and to act without compulsion on or from its sisters. Permissive legislation is more desirable anyway, for each city can act without awaiting the time when others all concur.

The writer will be glad to put any interested group in any city in touch with agencies which will gladly aid and collaborate in effecting the suggested reform.

However long may be the period over which the change is spread, first legislation should go all the way, for fickle change is dangerous. Benefits wil be cumulative and not too much should be expected in first stages. Pittsburgh's experience shows that much good will result long before the change is complete, and the assurance that ultimately a city will go all the way will give a sense of security and confidence to those who would build.

Legislation should be framed to cover all taxes levied on urban realty. There is often a state tax and nearly always some overlapping of city and county taxation. Generally, school taxes are a thing apart from the regular municipal levy and frequently there are special districts of one kind and another. Under the plan outlined, assessments are unchanged, and where a unit other than the city imposes a realty tax, it should be levied against the city on the basis of assessments perhaps corrected by equalization figures, to be added to the city budget and then re-collected and allocated in whatever manner the city accepts.

Some Specific Suggestions

The first objective should be the transfer to land values of the entire burden now placed on improvements. But there are details not to be overlooked. Set a ceiling on building assessments at present levels, permitting any justified reduction, but no increase. Experience shows that this is necessary to prevent manipulation, and it will give incentive to construction and rebuilding. Provide that any owner who so elects may immediately place his taxation on the basis to be established on completion of the change, if such action wil not reduce his present bill. This will give immediate inducement to improvement and will stabilize city revenue. In the case of a vacant lot paying $20, the owner may have his bill jumped at once to $60 (using Albany figures), with freedom to build without further increase, and this increase will not bother him if his $15,000 house, which would today be taxed $670, goes tax-free. Note, too, that while he is far better off, with the values of his property restored, the city will collect three times as much as it now tries unsuccessfully to collect. The owner now considering razing his building to cut tax costs will continue to let it stand and bring in revenue, pending the opportunity to replace it with a better structure, for the building will be no factor in tax costs. Many an Albany lot in process of forfeiture would be restored to the tax books could the owner look forward to a day when building would become possible and profitable.

Having gone thus far, we can then proceed to progressive increase in ground rents until the city shall recover its full rightful income. This increase in city revenue will pave the way to the abolition of other objectionable levies, such as the city sales tax, taxes on the conduct of business or the practice of a profession, and the most unfair personal property tax. There is often another tax, which, although we may not see it as such, is as truly an impost on improvements as is the direct city realty tax. Some states have a mortgage tax, generally shared by state and cities or districts concerned. However phrased, and regardless of who ostensibly pays it, it comes out of the borrower, and there is neither wisdom nor justice in penalizing borrowing to build the homes and the factories which make the city. Whatever it yields might far better be included in the regular tax on realty. It may take time to secure the repeal of this tax, and revision of direct city taxation should not be deferred until this is

[98]

accomplished, but it is a goal to be kept in view. The principle of a state law imposing state-collected taxes to be used for local purposes by local governments is unsound. There is nothing to be said for the state imposing an iniquitous local tax and then turning back the revenue to each locality, nor can such a law be defended on the slippery grounds that it enables a city to circumvent a tax-limitation law.

Coupled with this basic legislation should go other reforms discussed, making it easier and cheaper for a city to take title when taxes remain unpaid, although they will be far less of a problem with delinquency reduced. Provision should also be made permitting the city to hold forfeited properties, leasing them for ground rent instead of making demoralizing forced sales, and excess condemnation should be strengthened and more generally practiced.

A Broader View

Our argument has been primarily of economic principles and of practical benefits, but it has a deeper aspect. Does a creed that the earth, the first necessity of life, was given to be monopolized by a few to the exclusion of the many square with our ideas of the fatherhood of God and the brotherhood of man, or even with the most rudimentary concepts of fair dealing among men? Is it right that some should be denied all access to the source of all, without payment of tribute to others? Should not all share in this common gift of the Creator, not by dividing up, which would accomplish no good purpose, but by sharing a common heritage? And, conversely, does not respect for individual life and for the primary rights of "life, liberty and the pursuit of happiness" predicate our right to the full enjoyment of their fruits?

Since the support of government must be derived either through the collection of an income which justly belongs to all or by the confiscation of what is justly private property, *there is no other way in which we can be protected in the rights which are ours than the plan proposed.* The only alternative is the acceptance of the communistic doctrine that "property is theft" and the repudiation of the principles upon which our Republic was built. Substitute for taxation a just charge for benefits, advantages, services and values provided by the common life.

To seek a passing expediency at the expense of principles is to supersede justice by the faulty opinions of men, substituting human decisions for immutable laws. Such course can lead only to disaster. Doing right, we shall prosper and, leaving man's conscience free, we respect individuality and liberty. Men will be enabled to earn their livelihood in self-respect and self-reliance, and this is infinitely better than soul-destroying doles and humiliating charity exacted from others.

[99]

A thoughtful reader of this manuscript questions if enthusiasm does not lead us to anticipate too much. The only answer is that long years of study bring a broadening vision of possibilities and a growing confidence. Conviction is not a recent growth but the product of decades of open-minded consideration.

Perhaps we are oversanguine — but, "so what?" If we can eradicate only a few evils and curb only a few injustices, shall that hold us back? Fair dealing and right action must bring practical benefits, for if we believe that evil brings good and good works evil, all morality crumbles into dust. Doing right, we are content to leave results to the Power that shapes our lives, and if we earnestly seek the kingdom of heaven on earth, we shall find a better way of life.